I0004901

FORWARD/COMMENTARY

The National Institute of Standards and Technology (NIST) is a measurement standards laboratory, and a non-regulatory agency of the United States Department of Commerce. Its mission is to promote innovation and industrial competitiveness. Founded in 1901, as the National Bureau of Standards, NIST was formed with the mandate to provide standard weights and measures, and to serve as the national physical laboratory for the United States. With a world-class measurement and testing laboratory encompassing a wide range of areas of computer science, mathematics, statistics, and systems engineering, NIST's cybersecurity program supports its overall mission to promote U.S. innovation and industrial competitiveness by advancing measurement science, standards, and related technology through research and development in ways that enhance economic security and improve our quality of life.

The need for cybersecurity standards and best practices that address interoperability, usability and privacy has been shown to be critical for the nation. NIST's cybersecurity programs seek to enable greater development and application of practical, innovative security technologies and methodologies that enhance the country's ability to address current and future computer and information security challenges.

The cybersecurity publications produced by NIST cover a wide range of cybersecurity concepts that are carefully designed to work together to produce a holistic approach to cybersecurity primarily for government agencies and constitute the best practices used by industry. This holistic strategy to cybersecurity covers the gamut of security subjects from development of secure encryption standards for communication and storage of information while at rest to how best to recover from a cyber-attack.

Why buy a book you can download for free?

Some are available only in electronic media. Some online docs are missing pages or barely legible.

We at 4th Watch Books are former government employees, so we know how government employees actually use the standards. When a new standard is released, an engineer prints it out, punches holes and puts it in a 3-ring binder. While this is not a big deal for a 5 or 10-page document, many NIST documents are over 100 pages and printing a large document is a time-consuming effort. So, an engineer that's paid $75 an hour is spending hours simply printing out the tools needed to do the job. That's time that could be better spent doing engineering. We publish these documents so engineers can focus on what they were hired to do – engineering. It's much more cost-effective to just order the latest version from Amazon.com

If there is a standard you would like published, let us know. Our web site is Cybah.webplus.net

Please see the Cybersecurity Standards list at the end of this book.

CyberSecurity Standards Library™

Get a Complete Library of Over 300 Cybersecurity Standards on 1 Convenient DVD!

The **4th Watch CyberSecurity Standards Library** is a DVD disc that puts over 300 current and archived cybersecurity standards from NIST, DOD, DHS, CNSS and NERC at your fingertips! Many of these cybersecurity standards are hard to find and we included the current version and a previous version for many of them. The DVD includes four books written by Luis Ayala: **The Cyber Dictionary, Cybersecurity Standards**, **Cyber-Security Glossary of Building Hacks and Cyber-Attacks**, and **Cyber-Physical Attack Defenses: Preventing Damage to Buildings and Utilities**.

- ✓ DVD includes many Hard-to-find Cybersecurity Standards - some still in Draft.
- ✓ Docs are organized by source and listed numerically so each standard is easy to locate.
- ✓ The listing of standards on the DVD includes an abstract of the subject, and date issued.
- ✓ PDF format for use on PC, Mac, eReaders, or tablets.
- ✓ No need for WiFi / Internet.
- ✓ Save countless hours of searching and downloading.
- ✓ Carry in a briefcase - terrific for travel.

4th Watch Publishing is releasing the CyberSecurity Standards Library DVD to make it easier for you to access the tools you need to ensure the security of your computer networks and SCADA systems. We also publish many of these standards on demand so you don't need to waste valuable time searching for the latest version of a standard, printing hundreds of pages and punching holes so they can go in a three-ring binder. **Order on Amazon.com**

The DVD works on PC and Mac with the standards in PDF format. To view the CyberSecurity Standards Library on the DVD, a computer with a DVD drive is required. The most current version of your internet browser, at least 2GB of RAM, and current version of Adobe Reader is recommended. (Compatible browsers include Internet Explorer 8+, Mozilla Firefox 4+, Apple Safari 5+, Google Chrome 15+)

Draft NISTIR 8144

Assessing Threats to Mobile Devices & Infrastructure

The Mobile Threat Catalogue

Christopher Brown
Spike Dog
Joshua M Franklin
Neil McNab
Sharon Voss-Northrop
Michael Peck
Bart Stidham

National Institute of
Standards and Technology
U.S. Department of Commerce

Draft NISTIR 8144

Assessing Threats to Mobile Devices & Infrastructure

The Mobile Threat Catalogue

Joshua M Franklin
National Cybersecurity Center of Excellence
National Institute of Standards and Technology

Christopher Brown
Spike Dog
Neil McNab
Sharon Voss-Northrop
Michael Peck
The MITRE Corporation
McLean, VA

Bart Stidham
STS Mobile

September 2016

U.S. Department of Commerce
Penny Pritzker, Secretary

National Institute of Standards and Technology
Willie May, Under Secretary of Commerce for Standards and Technology and Director

49
50

National Institute of Standards and Technology Interagency Report 8144
50 pages (September 2016)

51

65

66

Public comment period: *September 12, 2016* through *October 12, 2016*

67
68
69
70

National Institute of Standards and Technology
Attn: Computer Security Division, Information Technology Laboratory
100 Bureau Drive (Mail Stop 8930) Gaithersburg, MD 20899-8930
Email: nistir8144@nist.gov

71

All comments are subject to release under the Freedom of Information Act (FOIA).

72

73   **Reports on Computer Systems Technology**

74   The Information Technology Laboratory (ITL) at the National Institute of Standards and
75   Technology (NIST) promotes the U.S. economy and public welfare by providing technical
76   leadership for the Nation's measurement and standards infrastructure. ITL develops tests, test
77   methods, reference data, proof of concept implementations, and technical analyses to advance the
78   development and productive use of information technology. ITL's responsibilities include the
79   development of management, administrative, technical, and physical standards and guidelines for
80   the cost-effective security and privacy of other than national security-related information in federal
81   information systems.

82   **Abstract**

83   Mobile devices pose a unique set of threats, yet typical enterprise protections fail to address the
84   larger picture. In order to fully address the threats presented by mobile devices, a wider view of
85   the mobile security ecosystem is necessary. This document discusses the *Mobile Threat*
86   *Catalogue*, which describes, identifies, and structures the threats posed to mobile information
87   systems.
88
89   **Keywords**

90   cellular security; enterprise mobility; mobility management; mobile; mobile device; mobile
91   security; mobile device management; telecommunications

92

93

94   **Acknowledgements**

95   The NCCoE and NIST would like to thank Michael Ogata and Andrew Regenscheid of NIST;
96   Vincent Sritapan of the Department of Homeland Security (DHS) Science & Technology
97   Directorate; and Kori Fisk and Mary Yang of MITRE for their contributions to this document.

98   **Note to Readers**

99   The development of this interagency report and the *Mobile Threat Catalogue* supports the *Study*
100   *on Mobile Device Security*, as a part of the Cybersecurity Act of 2015 - Title IV, Section 401.
101   Mobile threats and mitigations supporting the Congressional Study on Mobile Device Security
102   and the *Mobile Threat Catalogue* may incorporate submissions from request for information
103   (RFI) – Mobile Threats & Defenses from FedBizOps solicitation number: QTA00NS16SDI0003.

104   **Trademark Information**

105   All product names are registered trademarks or trademarks of their respective companies. The
106   Bluetooth logo is property of the Bluetooth Special Interest Group (SIG).

Table of Contents

1   Introduction 1

   1.1   Purpose 1

   1.2   Scope... 1

   1.3   Audience 2

   1.4   Document Structure 2

   1.5   Document Conventions... 2

2   Mobile Device & Infrastructure Attack Surface 3

   2.1   Mobile Technology Stack 3

   2.2   Communication Mechanisms.. 5

      2.2.1   Subscriber Identity Module (SIM) 5

      2.2.2   Cellular Air Interface 6

      2.2.3   WiFi 6

      2.2.4   Global Navigation Satellite System (GNSS) 7

      2.2.5   Bluetooth 7

      2.2.6   Near Field Communication (NFC) 7

      2.2.7   Secure Digital (SD) Card 7

      2.2.8   Power & Synchronization Port 8

   2.3   Supply Chain 8

   2.4   Mobile Ecosystem.. 8

      2.4.1   Cellular Infrastructure 9

      2.4.2   Public Application Stores.. 9

      2.4.3   Private Application Stores 10

      2.4.4   Device & OS Vendor Infrastructure 10

      2.4.5   Enterprise Mobility Management Systems 10

      2.4.6   Enterprise Mobile Services 10

3   Mobile Threat Catalogue 11

   3.1   Methodology 11

   3.2   Catalogue Structure... 11

   3.3   Category Descriptions.. 12

      3.3.1   Mobile Device Technology Stack 12

      3.3.2   Network Protocols, Technologies, and Infrastructure 13

139   3.3.3 Authentication.. 14

140   3.3.4 Supply Chain 15

141   3.3.5 Physical Access 15

142   3.3.6 Ecosystem 15

143   3.3.7 Enterprise Mobility 15

144   3.3.8 Payment 16

145   3.4 Next Steps 16

146
147   **List of Appendices**

148 **Appendix A— Acronyms** **17**

149 **Appendix B— References** **19**

150 **Appendix C— Mobile Threat Catalogue References** **21**

151
152   **List of Figures**

153 Figure 1 - Mobile Device Technology Stack 4

154 Figure 2 - Mobile Device Communication Mechanisms.................................... 5

155 Figure 3 - Mobile Ecosystem 9

156

157 **1   Introduction**

158   Mobile devices pose a unique set of threats to enterprises. Typical enterprise protections, such as
159   isolated enterprise sandboxes and the ability to remote wipe a device, may fail to fully mitigate
160   the security challenges associated with these complex mobile information systems. With this in
161   mind, a set of security controls and countermeasures that address mobile threats in a holistic
162   manner must be identified, necessitating a broader view of the entire mobile security ecosystem.
163   This view must go beyond devices to include, as an example, the cellular networks and cloud
164   infrastructure used to support mobile applications and native mobile services.

165   **1.1   Purpose**

166   This document outlines a catalogue of threats to mobile devices and associated mobile
167   infrastructure to support development and implementation of mobile security capabilities, best
168   practices, and security solutions to better protect enterprise information technology (IT). Threats
169   are divided into broad categories, primarily focused upon mobile applications and software, the
170   network stack and associated infrastructure, mobile device and software supply chain, and the
171   greater mobile ecosystem. Each threat identified is catalogued alongside explanatory and
172   vulnerability information where possible, and alongside applicable mitigation strategies.
173   Background information on mobile systems and their attack surface is provided to assist readers
174   in understanding threats contained within the Mobile Threat Catalogue (MTC). Readers are
175   encouraged to take advantage of resources identified and referenced within the MTC for more
176   detailed information, all of which are also referenced within Appendix C of this document.

177   The MTC is a separate document located at the Computer Security Resource Center (CSRC) [1].

178   **1.2   Scope**

179   NIST Special Publication (SP) 800-53 [10] defines a mobile device as:

180   "A portable computing device that: (i) has a small form factor such that it can easily be
181   carried by a single individual; (ii) is designed to operate without a physical connection
182   (e.g., wirelessly transmit or receive information); (iii) possesses local, non-removable or
183   removable data storage; and (iv) includes a self-contained power source. Mobile devices
184   may also include voice communication capabilities, on-board sensors that allow the
185   devices to capture information, and/or built-in features for synchronizing local data with
186   remote locations. Examples include smart phones, tablets, and E-readers."

187   With this definition in mind, smart phones and tablets running modern mobile operating systems
188   are the primary target of this analysis. Devices typically classified within the Internet of Things
189   (IoT) category are excluded from the scope of this document. Although some devices contain
190   capabilities to communicate via the auxiliary port and infrared, these are also excluded from the
191   scope of this effort as they are not common methods of attack.

192   Cellular networks are prominently featured within the catalogue, and accordingly comprise a
193   large portion of this document's information. However, although cellular networks are becoming
194   increasingly intertwined with the internet and private packet switched networks, internet protocol
195   (IP) network security is covered extensively by other resources and not within the scope of this

196 work. Finally, threats specific to the Public Switched Telephone Network (PSTN) are also
197 excluded.

1.3   Audience

199 Mobile security engineers and architects can leverage this document to inform risk assessments,
200 build threat models, enumerate the attack surface of their mobile infrastructure, and identify
201 mitigations for their mobile deployments. Other audiences for this document include mobile
202 operating system (OS) developers, device manufacturers, mobile network operators (MNOs)
203 (e.g., carriers), mobile application developers and information system security professionals who
204 are responsible for managing the mobile devices in an enterprise environment.

205 This document may also be useful when developing enterprise-wide procurement and
206 deployment strategies for mobile devices and when evaluating the risk mobile devices pose to
207 otherwise secure parts of the enterprise. The material in this document is technically oriented,
208 and it is assumed that readers have an understanding of system and network security.

1.4   Document Structure

210 The remainder of this document is organized into the following major sections:

211   • Section 2 provides a background on the attack surface of mobile devices and their
212   associated infrastructure.
213   • Section 3 details the structure of the MTC and the methodology used to create it.

214 The document also contains appendices with supporting material:

215   • Appendix A defines selected acronyms and abbreviations used in this publication,
216   • Appendix B contains a list of references used in the development of this document, and
217   • Appendix C contains a list of references from the MTC.

1.5   Document Conventions

219 The following conventions are used throughout the Interagency Report:

220   • This work is not specific to a given mobile platform or operating system (OS). Most
221   identified threats are agnostic to a specific platform; however, the catalogue specifically
222   distinguishes any instance where that is not the case.
223   • All products and services mentioned are owned by their respective organizations.

224   ## 2   Mobile Device & Infrastructure Attack Surface

225   The functionality provided by mobile devices has significantly evolved over the past two
226   decades and continues to rapidly advance. When first introduced, mobile devices were basic
227   cellular phones designed to make telephone calls. Although carriers were targeted by malicious
228   actors wanting to make free phone calls, users and their data were rarely the target of criminals.
229   Once modern mobile OSs were introduced over a decade later, the threat landscape drastically
230   changed as users began trusting these devices with large quantities of sensitive personal
231   information. Enterprises also started allowing employees to use mobile devices and applications
232   to access enterprise email, contacts, and calendar functionality. Shortly after the wide scale
233   adoption of modern smartphones, a large upscale in the use and deployment of cloud services
234   occurred. While this reduced costs and simplified operations for businesses, it altered the threat
235   landscape in its own unique way.

236   The following sections describe primary components of the mobile attack surface: mobile device
237   technology stack, mobile and local network protocol stacks, supply chain, and the greater mobile
238   ecosystem.

239   ### 2.1   Mobile Technology Stack

240   Mobile devices share some architectural similarities with their desktop counterparts, but there are
241   significant distinctions between personal computers and these portable information systems. In
242   addition to cellular functionality, including a number of radios, modern smartphones and tablets
243   typically include a full suite of environmental sensors, cryptographic processors, and multiple
244   wireless and wired communication methods. They also include a touch screen, audio interface,
245   one or more high definition (HD) video cameras, and in odd edge cases unusual capabilities like
246   video projectors.

247   Figure 1 illustrates the mobile device technology stack, described in additional detail further
248   below.

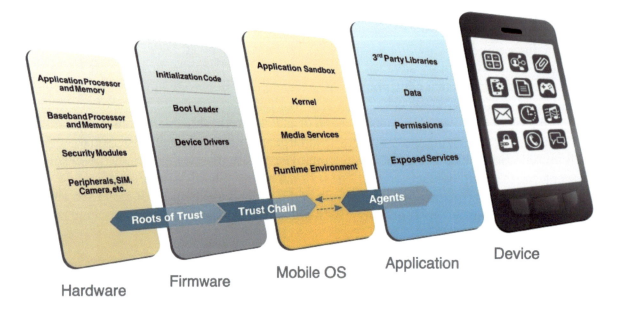

249

250   **Figure 1 - Mobile Device Technology Stack**

251

252   For smart phones and tablets with cellular capabilities, a separation exists between the hardware
253   and firmware used to access cellular networks and the hardware and firmware used to operate the
254   general purpose mobile OS. The hardware and firmware used to access the cellular network,
255   often referred to as the telephony subsystem, typically runs a real-time operating system (RTOS).
256   This telephony subsystem is colloquially named the *baseband processor,* and may be
257   implemented on a dedicated System on a Chip (SoC), or included as part of the SoC containing
258   the application processor also running the general purpose mobile OS.

259   The firmware necessary to boot the mobile OS (i.e., bootloader) may verify additional device
260   initialization code, device drivers used for peripherals, and portions of the mobile OS – all before
261   a user can use the device. If the initialization code is modified or tampered with in some manner,
262   the device may not properly function. Many modern mobile devices contain an isolated
263   execution environment, which are used specifically for security-critical functions [7]. For
264   example, these environments may be used for sensitive cryptographic operations, to verify
265   integrity, or to support Digital Rights Management. These environments typically have access to
266   some amount of secure storage which is only accessible within that environment.

267   The mobile OS enables a rich set of functionality by supporting the use of mobile applications
268   written by third-party developers. Accordingly, it is common for mobile applications to be
269   sandboxed in some manner to prevent unexpected and unwanted interaction between the system,
270   its applications, and those applications' respective data (including user data). Mobile applications
271   may be written in native code running closely to the hardware, in interpreted languages, or in
272   high-level web languages. The degree of functionality of mobile applications is highly dependent

273   upon the application programming interfaces (APIs) exposed by the mobile OS.[1]

2.2   Communication Mechanisms

275   Contemporary mobile devices contain integrated hardware components to support a variety of
276   I/O mechanisms. While some of the communication mechanisms are wireless (i.e., cellular,
277   WiFi, Bluetooth, GPS, NFC), others require a physical connection (i.e., power and
278   synchronization cable, SIM, external storage). As seen in Figure 2, each of these different
279   wireless and wired device communication mechanisms exposes the device to a distinct set of
280   threats and must be secured or the overall security of the device may be compromised.

281

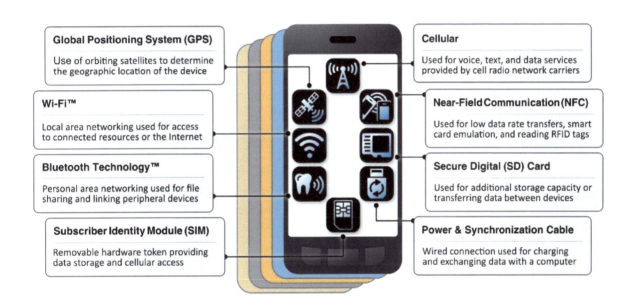

283   **Figure 2 - Mobile Device Communication Mechanisms**

284   The following sections provide a brief overview of each communication mechanism.

2.2.1   Subscriber Identity Module (SIM)

286   This removable hardware token is colloquially referred to as the Subscriber Identity Module
287   (SIM) card, although current standards use the term Universal Integrated Circuit Card (UICC).
288   This System on a Chip (SoC) houses the subscriber identity (i.e., International Mobile Subscriber
289   Identity), pre-shared cryptographic keys, and configuration information needed to obtain access
290   to cellular networks. The UICC is essentially a smartcard that runs a Java application known as
291   the Universal Subscriber Identity Module (USIM), which is used to run a set of applications that
292   control the phone's access and authentication with the MNO's cellular networks and roaming
293   partners. It is possible to develop and run other applications on the Java Card platform, such as

---

[1] For additional information about mobile application security, see NIST SP 800-163 – Vetting the Security of Mobile
    Applications [5].

294   games and mobile payment applications.

295   As of the writing of this Interagency Report, a technology called Embedded SIM (eSIM) is being
296   integrated into some mobile devices [4]. eSIMs will allow MNOs to remotely provision
297   subscriber information during initial device setup, and allow the remote changing of subscription
298   from one MNO to another. While this technology may radically change the way mobile devices
299   are provisioned on the carrier network and therefore introduces a new set of threats.

2.2.2   Cellular Air Interface

301   The cellular air interface is arguably the defining networking interface for modern mobile
302   devices. Initial cellular systems, such as second generation (2G) Global System for Mobile
303   Communications (GSM) and third generation (3G) Universal Mobile Telecommunications
304   System, were modeled after the traditional wireline circuit-switched telephone system. Each call
305   was provided with a dedicated circuit providing a user making a telephone call with a baseline
306   guarantee of service. In contrast, newer fourth generation (4G) Long Term Evolution (LTE)
307   networks were designed to utilize a packet-switched model for both data and voice. An LTE
308   network provides consistent IP connectivity between an end user's mobile device and IP-based
309   services on the packet data network (PDN).

310   There are many cellular network types, each with its own air interface standards. The cellular air
311   interface is the technical term for the radio connection between a mobile device and the cellular
312   tower. This air interface can generally communicate with many types of base stations (e.g.,
313   cellular towers) which come in many sizes and types — cellular repeater / relay nodes, and even
314   other handsets.

315   MNOs strive to run high availability "carrier grade" services that operate over the air interface at
316   the network level, and can integrate with other systems they operate. These services may include
317   circuit switched calling, VoLTE (Voice over LTE), Unstructured Supplementary Service Data
318   (USSD), integrated voicemail with notifications, and messaging (e.g., Short Messaging Service
319   (SMS)). Carrier-grade messaging services are commonly referred to as text messages, but
320   include SMS, the extension to SMS known as Multimedia Messaging Service (MMS), and the
321   new Rich Communication Services (RCS). USSD is an aging method for establishing a real-time
322   session with a service or application to quickly share short messages. Although not common
323   within the United States, USSD is used in emerging markets for a number of services, including
324   mobile banking.

325   For additional discussion of LTE security architecture see NISTIR 8071 – LTE Architecture
326   Overview and Security Analysis [16].

2.2.3   WiFi

328   WiFi is a wireless local area network (WLAN) technology based on the IEEE 802.11 series of
329   standards. WiFi is used by most mobile devices as an alternative to cellular data channels, or
330   even the primary data egress point in WiFi-only mobile devies. WLANs typically consist of a
331   group of wireless devices within a contained physical area, such as an apartment, office, or
332   coffee shop, but more expansive enterprise or campus deployments are also common. While not
333   guaranteed, campus or enterprise deployments are more likely to implement security features

334 such as WPA2 encryption. Smartphones, laptops, and other devices utilizing WiFi often need to
335 connect back to a central wireless access point (APs), but may work in a device-to-device *ad hoc*
336 mode.

337 Readers looking for additional guidance for the installation, configuration, deployment, and
338 security of WiFi can see NIST SP 800-153 – Guidelines for Securing Wireless Local Area
339 Networks [14] or SP 800-97 – Establishing Wireless Robust Security Networks: A Guide to
340 IEEE 802.11i [15].

341 **2.2.4   Global Navigation Satellite System (GNSS)**

342 A GNSS provides worldwide geo-spatial positioning via the global positioning system (GPS),
343 which uses line of sight communication with a satellite constellation in orbit to help a handset
344 determine its location. These systems run independently of cellular networks. The US Federal
345 Government operates a GPS constellation, although mobile devices may use other systems (e.g.,
346 GLONASS, Galileo). It should be noted that the GPS system is not the only way for a mobile
347 device to identify its location. Other techniques include Wi-Fi assisted positioning, which
348 leverages databases of known service set identifiers (SSIDs) and geolocation of IP addresses.

349 **2.2.5   Bluetooth**

350 Bluetooth is a short-range wireless communication technology. Bluetooth technology is used
351 primarily to establish wireless personal area networks (PANs). Bluetooth technology has been
352 integrated into many types of business and consumer devices including cell phones, laptops,
353 automobiles, medical devices, printers, keyboards, mice, headphones, and headsets. This allows
354 users to form *ad hoc* networks between a wide variety of devices to transfer data.

355 For additional information about Bluetooth security, see NIST SP 800-121 Revision 1 – Guide to
356 Bluetooth Security [13].

357 **2.2.6   Near Field Communication (NFC)**

358 NFC uses radio frequency emissions to establish low throughput, short-range communication
359 between NFC-enabled devices. It is typically optimized for distances of less than 4 inches, but
360 can potentially operate at and pose a threat at much greater distances. NFC is based on the radio
361 frequency identification (RFID) set of standards. Mobile payment technology relies on NFC,
362 which has led to NFC's increasing visibility in recent years as newer mobile wallet technologies
363 are being deployed on a large scale. The use of NFC for financial transactions make it attractive
364 to criminal attackers with the goal of financial gain.

365 For additional information on the security challenges associated with RFID, refer to NIST SP
366 800-98 – Guidelines for Securing Radio Frequency Identification (RFID) Systems [12].

367 **2.2.7   Secure Digital (SD) Card**

368 The SD card standard comprises various form factors that offer different performance ratings and
369 storage capacities. SD cards are typically used to expand the storage capacity of mobile devices
370 to store data such as photos, videos, music, and application data. SD cards are not integrated into

371 every mobile device, although the use of SD cards is particularly popular in developing nations
372 where built-in storage may be uncommon.

373 2.2.8 Power & Synchronization Port

374 The power and synchronization port on a mobile device is most often used to charge a mobile
375 device, and may take the form of Universal Serial Bus (USB) Type-C, Micro-USB, Apple
376 Lightning, or Apple 30 pin. The cable is also used to carry data to, or access the device from,
377 another information system. Use cases include data synchronization with or backup to a PC, or
378 provisioning into an Enterprise Mobility Management system. This cable may also be used to
379 charge another device in some circumstances. Because of this dual use of power *and data*, this
380 interface is used as a vector for a number of attacks.

381 2.3 Supply Chain

382 Mobile devices are designed, manufactured, distributed, used, and disposed of in a manner
383 similar to other commercial electronics. Unique threats to mobile devices exist at every part of
384 this lifecycle. Supply chain threats are particularly difficult to mitigate because mobile device
385 components are under constant development and are sourced from tens of thousands of original
386 equipment manufacturers (OEMs). Some subcomponents of mobile devices (e.g., baseband
387 processors) require matched firmware developed by the OEM. This firmware can itself contain
388 software vulnerabilities and can increase the overall attack surface of the mobile device.

389 Of the layers presented in the mobile device technology stack featured in Figure 1, a variety of
390 different organizations own or control different parts. In the case of Apple's highly vertically
391 integrated iOS devices, Apple develops the mobile operating system, as well as the majority of
392 the specialized firmware and hardware components. In contrast, Google's Android ecosystem is
393 almost completely vertically sliced with both hardware and software components being supplied
394 by tens of thousands of vendors. Google does not manufacture any hardware components,
395 although they do form partnerships to create the Google-branded Nexus series of Android
396 reference devices. An independent handset manufacturer may design a majority of the hardware
397 and firmware to operate an Android device, and even customize the Android user interface;
398 however, they still need Google's core Android OS to be part of the massive Android application
399 ecosystem. This entire design and manufacturing process has the potential to markedly influence
400 the security architecture of the resulting mobile device.

401 2.4 Mobile Ecosystem

402 Mobile devices do not exist in a vacuum - a series networks and interconnected systems exist to
403 support modern mobility. The utility of modern mobile devices is greatly enhanced by software
404 applications and their supporting cloud services. Mobile OSs provide dedicated application
405 stores for end users offering a convenient and customized means of adding functionality.
406 Application stores pose an additional threat vector for attackers to distribute malware or other
407 harmful software to end users. This is especially true of third-party application stores not directly
408 supervised by mobile OS vendors.

409 Mobile applications may traverse many networks and interact with systems owned and operated

410   by many parties to accomplish their intended goals. This mobile ecosystem is depicted in the
411   Figure 3.

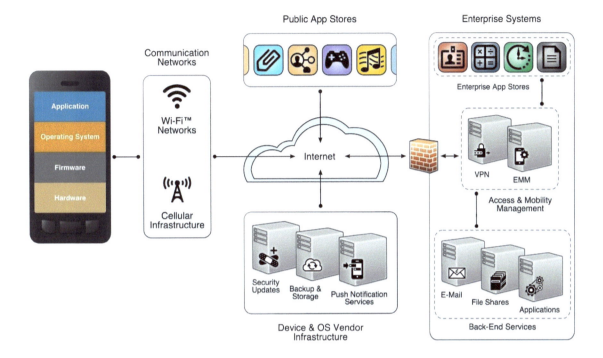

412

413   **Figure 3 - Mobile Ecosystem**

414   **2.4.1   Cellular Infrastructure**

415   MNOs build out cellular base stations over a large geographic area. These base stations modulate
416   and demodulate radio signals to communicate with mobile devices. Base stations forward mobile
417   device information, such as calls, messages, and other data, to other base stations and a cellular
418   network core. The cellular network core contains anchor points to communicate with other
419   networks, such as other MNO's cellular networks, WiFi networks, the Internet, and the PSTN.
420   Cellular network cores also rely upon authentication servers to use and store customer
421   authentication information.

422   **2.4.2   Public Application Stores**

423   Major mobile operating vendors own and operate their own native mobile application stores,
424   which host mobile applications for users to download and install. These stores also provide
425   music, movies, video games, and more. Access to these stores is natively installed and
426   configured into mobile devices. Third-party mobile application stores also exist for most mobile
427   operating systems. These third-party application stores may be explicitly built into the mobile
428   OS, or they may be added as additional functionality for jailbroken or rooted devices.[2] Third-

---

[2] Jailbreaking or rooting a mobile device bypasses built-in restrictions on security. While this may provide the user more freedom
to control their device, at the same time may compromise the security architecture of the mobile device.

429 party application stores may be completely legitimate, but may also host applications that
430 commit substantial copyright violations or "cracked" versions of applications that allow users to
431 install and use paid applications for free.

432 The native application stores are hosted and operated by their respective mobile OS developers.

433 2.4.3 Private Application Stores

434 Many enterprises and other organizations host their own mobile application stores. These stores
435 either host, or link to, a set of applications for an organization's users to access. These
436 applications may be privately developed applications that organizations do not wish to be made
437 public, or they may be publicly available applications that have been specifically approved for
438 enterprise use. The servers used to host these applications may be privately hosted and operated
439 by the enterprise, or hosted and operated by a third-party cloud provider.

440 2.4.4 Device & OS Vendor Infrastructure

441 Mobile OS developers often host infrastructure to provide updates and patches to a mobile
442 device's OS and native applications. Other cloud-based applications may be provided as well,
443 including functionality to locate, lock, or wipe a missing device or to store user data (e.g.,
444 pictures, notes, music).

445 2.4.5 Enterprise Mobility Management Systems

446 Enterprise Mobility Management (EMM) systems are a common way of managing mobile
447 devices in an enterprise. Although EMMs are not directly classified as a security technology,
448 they can help to deploy policies to an enterprise's device pool and to monitor a device's state.
449 Mobile OS developers provide APIs for EMM systems to deliver mobile policies, such as only
450 allowing a whitelisted set of applications to run; ensuring a lock screen security policy is met;
451 and disabling certain device peripherals (e.g., camera). EMMs can also use APIs to gather data
452 about various aspects of a mobile device's state.

453 For more information about the management and security of EMMs, see NIST SP 800-124 –
454 Guidelines for Managing the Security of Mobile Devices in the Enterprise [2].

455 2.4.6 Enterprise Mobile Services

456 Email, contacts, and calendars are common workforce drivers, and are the cornerstone
457 applications in mobile devices that are deployed by enterprises. Directory services are also
458 deployed in an enterprise and used by mobile devices. Enterprises may also make other services
459 available to mobile devices depending on their specific mission needs and requirements..

460

461 **3   Mobile Threat Catalogue**

462   The MTC captures a broad range of the threats posed to mobile devices and their associated
463   infrastructure. The following section describes the structure of the catalogue and the
464   methodology used to create it.

465   **3.1   Methodology**

466   NCCoE's mobile security engineers performed a foundational review of mobile security
467   literature in order to identify major categories of mobile threats. Building upon this knowledge,
468   threats were identified using a modified NIST SP 800-30 risk assessment process [6]. One of the
469   primary drivers for change was the lack of a specific information system under review. A single
470   mobile deployment was not under review – instead the threats posed to foundational mobile
471   technologies were analyzed. Therefore, key risk information necessitated by NIST SP 800-30
472   such as likelihood, impact, and overall risk was unavailable and not included. Threats were
473   identified in communication mechanisms, the mobile supply chain, and at each level of the
474   mobile device technology stack. These threats were then placed into threat categories alongside
475   information pertaining to specific instantiations of these threats.

476   During the threat identification process, it was necessary to identify which associated systems
477   would be included and applicable mitigation capabilities. The mitigation capabilities are
478   inclusive of a mobile security literature review and submissions resulting from the request for
479   information on mobile threats and defenses[3], which support the congressional study on mobile
480   device security. A broad scope was used in an effort to be comprehensive. The threats listed in
481   the catalogue are sector-agnostic. For instance, threats pertaining to the use of mobile devices in
482   a medical setting are not included. The exception to this is the inclusion of threats pertaining to
483   the telecommunications industry, since this includes threats to cellular networks and
484   infrastructure by definition.

485   **3.2   Catalogue Structure**

486   Threats are presented in categories and subcategories within the catalogue. NIST 800-30
487   Revision 1 defines a threat as "any circumstance or event with the potential to adversely impact
488   organizational operations and assets, individuals, other organizations, or the Nation through an
489   information system via unauthorized access, destruction, disclosure, or modification of
490   information, and/or denial of service" [6]. For each threat identified within our analysis, the
491   following information is provided:

492   •   **Threat Category:** The major topic area pertaining to this threat. Topic areas are further
493   divided when necessary, and are discussed in section 3.3.

494   •   **Threat Identifier (ID):** The Threat ID is a unique identifier for referencing a specific
495   threat. The broad identifier categories used within the MTC are:

---

[3] FedBizOps solicitation number: QTA00NSTS16SDI0003

496   o   *APP*: Application

497   o   *STA*: Stack

498   o   *CEL*: Cellular

499   o   *GPS*: Global Positioning System

500   o   *LPN*: Local Area Network & Personal Area Network

501   o   *AUT*: Authentication

502   o   *SPC*: Supply Chain

503   o   *PHY*: Physical

504   o   *ECO*: Ecosystem

505   o   *EMM*: Enterprise Mobility Management

506   o   *PAY*: Payment

507   • **Threat Origin**: Reference to the source material used to initially identify the threat.

508   • **Exploit Example**: A reference to the vulnerability's origin or examples of specific
509   instances of this threat.

510   • **Common Vulnerability and Exposure (CVE) Reference**: A specific vulnerability
511   located within the National Vulnerability Database (NVD) [10]. A vulnerability origin
512   may describe a specific vulnerability, which may, or may not, be associated with a CVE.

513   • **Possible Countermeasure**: Security controls or mitigations that could reduce the impact
514   of a particular threat. If a countermeasure is not present, it may be an area for future
515   research.

516   The CVE is a dictionary of publicly known information security vulnerabilities and exposures
517   [11].

518   ## 3.3   Category Descriptions

519   There are 12 tabs within the MTC, each acting as general threat categories with subcategories
520   defined as necessary.

521   ### 3.3.1   Mobile Device Technology Stack

522   As discussed in Section 2.1, the mobile device technology stack consists of the hardware,
523   firmware, and software used to host and operate the mobile device.

524   • Mobile Applications: The Applications tab contains threats related to software

525   application developed for a mobile device, or more specifically a mobile operating
526   system. *Note: The Applications category was separated into its own tab to enhance the*
527   *usability of the catalogue. All of the other items are listed under the Stack tab.*

528   o   Vulnerable Applications: This subcategory contains threats related to discrete
529   software vulnerabilities residing within mobile applications running on top the
530   mobile operating system. *Note: Some vulnerabilities may be specific to a*
531   *particular mobile OS, while others may be generally applicable.*

532   o   Malicious or Privacy-Invasive Applications: This subcategory identifies mobile
533   malware based threats, based in part on Google's mobile classification taxonomy
534   [3]. There are no specific software vulnerabilities within this subcategory, and
535   accordingly no CVEs are cited. Additional malware categories are included
536   within subcategory to augment Google's classification taxonomy.

537   •   Mobile Operating System: Operating system specifically designed for a mobile device
538   and running mobile applications.

539   •   Device Drivers: Plug-ins used to interact with device hardware and other peripherals
540   (e.g., camera, accelerometer).

541   •   Isolated Execution Environments: Hardware or firmware-based environment built into
542   the mobile device that may provide many capabilities such as trusted key storage, code
543   verification, code integrity, and trusted execution for security relevant processes.

544   •   SD Card: SD cards are removable memory used to expand the storage capacity of mobile
545   devices to store data such as photos, videos, music, and application data.

546   •   Boot Firmware: The firmware necessary to boot the mobile OS (i.e., bootloader).
547   Firmware may verify additional device initialization code, device drivers used for
548   peripherals, and portions of the mobile OS – all before a user can use the device.

549   •   Baseband Subsystem: The collection of hardware and firmware used to communicate
550   with the cellular network via the cellular radio.

551   •   SIM Card: This removable hardware token is a SoC housing the IMSI, pre-shared
552   cryptographic keys, and configuration information needed to obtain access to cellular
553   networks.

554   **3.3.2 Network Protocols, Technologies, and Infrastructure**

555   Although divided into multiple sections within the mobile threat catalogue, this category
556   includes wireless protocols and technologies used by mobile devices.

557   •   Cellular: Threats exist to a number of cellular systems, broken into the following
558   subcategories:

559   o   Air Interface: The cellular air interface is the radio connection between a handset

560   and a base station. There are many cellular network types each with its own air
561   interface standards which as a total set are extremely flexible and primarily
562   communicate with base stations. *Note: While a number of general threats to the*
563   *cellular air interface are listed, specific threats to particular cellular protocols*
564   *(e.g., GSM, CDMA, LTE) are also included.*

565   o Consumer grade small cell: Small cells are often used to extend cellular network
566   coverage into homes, offices, and other locations lacking service.

567   o Carrier-grade Messaging Services: Messaging services (i.e., SMS, MMS, RCS)
568   allow text, photos, and more to be sent from one device to another. Although
569   third-party messaging services exist, carrier-grade messaging services are pre-
570   installed on nearly every mobile phone, and are interoperable with most MNOs'
571   networks.

572   o USSD: A method for establishing real-time sessions with a service or application
573   to quickly share short messages. Although USSD messages may travel over SMS,
574   the protocol itself is distinct.

575   o Carrier Infrastructure: This category includes threats to the base stations, backhaul
576   and cellular network cores.

577   o Carrier Interoperability: This subcategory is primarily reserved for signaling
578   threats associated with the Signaling System No. 7 (SS7) network.

579   o VoLTE: The packet switched network application used for making voice calls
580   within LTE. Although not supported in all MNO networks, large-scale rollouts
581   are underway throughout the world.

582   • LAN & PAN: This threat category consists of local and personal area wireless network
583   technologies.

584   o WiFi: WiFi is a WLAN technology based on the IEEE 802.11 series of standards.

585   o Bluetooth: Bluetooth is a medium-range, lower power, wireless communication
586   technology.

587   o NFC: NFC is a short range wireless communication technology commonly used
588   for mobile wallet technologies and peripheral configuration, although a number of
589   other applications exist.

590   • GPS: A network of orbiting satellites used to help a device determine its location.

591   ### 3.3.3 Authentication

592   Authentication mechanisms are grouped within the three subcategories listed below. Individual
593   credential and token types are not broken into their own categories and are instead included
594   within one of these three broad categories.

595 • User to Device: Mechanisms used to authenticate with a mobile device, such as
596   passwords, fingerprints, or voice recognition. This is most often local authentication to a
597   device's lock screen.

598 • User or Device to Remote Service: Mechanisms a user or a distinct non-person entity
599   (NPE) uses to remotely authenticate to an external process, service, or device.

600 • User or Device to Network: Mechanisms a user, mobile device, or peripheral uses to
601   authenticate to a network (e.g., Wi-Fi, cellular). This commonly includes proving
602   possession of a cryptographic token.

603 ### 3.3.4 Supply Chain

604 This category includes threats related to the device and component supply chain. To the extent
605 that they are included, software supply chain related threats are noted within the Exploitation of
606 Vulnerabilities in Applications category.

607 ### 3.3.5 Physical Access

608 This category includes general threats originating from outside of the device, such as device loss
609 and malicious charging stations.

610 ### 3.3.6 Ecosystem

611 This category includes threats related to the greater mobile ecosystem includes a number of
612 items, including EMMs, mobile OS vendor infrastructure, and mobile enterprise services such as
613 email, contacts, and calendar.

614 • Mobile OS Vendor Infrastructure: Infrastructure provided by the OS developer to provide
615   OS and application updates, alongside auxiliary services such as cloud storage.

616 • Native Public Stores: Major mobile operating system vendors own and operate their own
617   native mobile application stores, which host mobile applications alongside music,
618   movies, games, etc. for users to download and install.

619 • Private Enterprise Stores: Application stores may be owned and operated by private
620   enterprises to host applications not meant for public distribution, such as applications
621   developed and used solely within the organization.

622 • Third-Party Stores: Other legitimate, and illegitimate, application stores may be owned
623   and operated by organizations external to the major mobile operating system vendors.

624 ### 3.3.7 Enterprise Mobility

625 This threat category comprises enterprise mobility management systems and threats to
626 enterprises services.

627   **3.3.8 Payment**

628   Threats related to mobile payments are included within this category, including a variety of
629   mobile payment technologies such as USSD, NFC-based payments, and credit card tokenization.
630   Although general threats relating to USSD and NFC are included elsewhere, threats relating to
631   payment specific use cases are captured here.

632   **3.4 Next Steps**

633   The NCCoE aims to construct a series of mobile security projects to address the threats listed in
634   the MTC. A subset of the threats listed in the MTC may be identified for each project. Example
635   projects could include mobile application vetting, mobile security for public safety handsets, and
636   cellular security for the LTE air interface. Additionally, the NCCoE has partnered with the Cyber
637   Security Division at the DHS Science & Technology Directorate in mobile security research for
638   future research and development to spur innovation. The list of mobile threats lacking mitigation
639   capabilities will be considered primary areas for future research and development projects in
640   mobile security.

641   The NCCoE is interested in receiving comments on the Mobile Threat Catalogue, ideas for
642   future mobile security projects, and mobile security architectures operating and/or managing
643   enterprise mobile deployments. The NCCoE is also interested in feedback from mobile
644   technology vendors who may wish to work in collaboration to solve mobile security challenges.
645   Please connect with the NCCoE's mobile security team at mobile-nccoe@nist.gov.

646   If you have specific comments on this document, please email us at nistir8144@nist.gov.

647 **Appendix A—Acronyms**

648   Selected acronyms and abbreviations used in this paper are defined below.

2G	2nd Generation
3G	3rd Generation
4G	4th Generation
AP	Access Point
API	Application Programming Interface
BYOD	Bring Your Own Device
COPE	Corporately Owned Personally Enabled
COTS	Commercially Available off the Shelf
CSRC	Computer Security Resource Center
CVE	Common Vulnerabilities & Exposures
DoS	Denial of Service
EMM	Enterprise Mobility Management
GNSS	Global Navigation Satellite System
GSM	Global System for Mobile Communications
FIPS	Federal Information Processing Standard
HD	High Definition
IoT	Internet of Things
IP	Internet Protocol
IT	Information Technology
LTE	Long Term Evolution
MDM	Mobile Device Management
MNO	Mobile Network Operator
MMS	Multimedia Messaging Service

MTC	Mobile Threat Catalogue
NCCoE	National Cybersecurity Center of Excellence
NFC	Near Field Communication
NIST	National Institute of Standards and Technology
NISTIR	NIST Interagency Report
NPE	Non-Person Entity
OS	Operating System
PAN	Personal Area network
PSTN	Public Switched Telephone Networks
RCS	Rich Communication Services
RFID	Radio Frequency Identification
SD	Secure Digital
SIG	Special Interest Group
SIM	Subscriber Identity Module
SMS	Short Message Service
SoC	System on a Chip
SP	Special Publication
SS7	Signaling System No. 7
SSID	Service Set Identifier
UICC	Universal Integrated Circuit Card
UMTS	Universal Mobile Telecommunications System
USIM	Universal Subscriber Identity Module
USSD	Unstructured Supplementary Service Data
VPN	Virtual Private Network
WLAN	Wireless Local Area Network

649 **Appendix B—References**

[1]   National Institute of Standards and Technology, *Computer Security Resource Center*, 2016. [web page]
        http://csrc.nist.gov [accessed 8/23/16].

[2]   M. Souppaya and K. Scarfone, *Guidelines for Managing the Security of Mobile Devices in the Enterprise,* NIST SP 800-124 Revision 1, NIST, June 2013.
        http://nvlpubs.nist.gov/nistpubs/SpecialPublications/NIST.SP.800-124r1.pdf
        [accessed 8/23/15].

[3]   Google, The Google Android Security Team's Classifications for Potentially Harmful Applications, April 2016.
        https://static.googleusercontent.com/media/source.android.com/en//security/reports/Google_Android_Security_PHA_classifications.pdf

[4]   GSMA, Embedded SIM Remote Provisioning Architecture, Version 1.1, December 2013.
        http://www.gsma.com/connectedliving/wp-content/uploads/2014/01/1.-GSMA-Embedded-SIM-Remote-Provisioning-Architecture-Version-1.1.pdf

[5]   S. Quirolgico et. al., *Vetting the Security of Mobile Applications,* NIST SP 800-163, NIST, January 2015.
        http://nvlpubs.nist.gov/nistpubs/SpecialPublications/NIST.SP.800-163.pdf

[6]   National Institute of Standards and Technology, Guide for Conducting Risk Assessments, NIST SP 800-30 Revision 1, NIST, September 2012.
        http://csrc.nist.gov/publications/nistpubs/800-30-rev1/sp800_30_r1.pdf

[7]   Mandt, Solnik, and Wang, *Demystifying the Secure Enclave Processor,* Blackhat 2016.
        https://www.blackhat.com/docs/us-16/materials/us-16-Mandt-Demystifying-The-Secure-Enclave-Processor.pdf

[8]   Delugré, Guillaume, *Reverse engineering a Qualcomm baseband,* Sogeti / ESEC R&D, 2011.
        https://events.ccc.de/congress/2011/Fahrplan/attachments/2022_11-ccc-qcombb

[9]   National Institute of Standards and Technology, *National Vulnerability Database,* 2015. http://nvd.nist.gov [accessed 9/2/2015].

[10]   National Institute of Standards and Technology, *Security and Privacy Controls for Federal Information Systems and Organizations*, NIST SP 800-53 Revision 4, April 2013. http://nvlpubs.nist.gov/nistpubs/SpecialPublications/NIST.SP.800-

53r4.pdf [accessed 9/9/15].

[11]   MITRE, *Common Vulnerabilities and Exposures*, 2016. [Web page]
            http://cve.mitre.org/ [accessed 8/22/2016]

[12]   T. Karygiannis, et al., *NIST SP 800-98 Guidelines for Securing Radio Frequency
            Identification (RFID) Systems*, National Institute of Standards and Technology,
            April 2007. http://csrc.nist.gov/publications/nistpubs/800-98/SP800-98_RFID-
            2007.pdf

[13]   J. Padgette, K. Scarfone, L. Chen, *NIST SP 800-121 Revision 1 – Guide to
            Bluetooth Security*, National Institute of Standards and Technology, June 2012.
            http://csrc.nist.gov/publications/nistpubs/800-121-rev1/sp800-121_rev1.pdf

[14]   M. Souppaya, K. Scarfone, *NIST SP 800-153 - Guidelines for Securing Wireless
            Local Area Networks (WLANs)*, National Institute of Standards and Technology,
            February 2012.
            http://nvlpubs.nist.gov/nistpubs/Legacy/SP/nistspecialpublication800-153.pdf

[15]   S. Frankel, B. Eydt, L. Owens, K. Scarfone, *NIST 800-97 - Establishing Wireless
            Robust Security Networks: A Guide to IEEE 802.11i*, National Institute of
            Standards and Technology, February 2007.
            http://csrc.nist.gov/publications/nistpubs/800-97/SP800-97.pdf

[16]   J. Cichonski, M. Bartock, J. Franklin, *NISTIR 8071 - LTE Architecture Overview
            and Security Analysis (DRAFT)*, NIST, April 2106.
            http://csrc.nist.gov/publications/drafts/nistir-8071/nistir_8071_draft.pdf

[17]   Google, *The Google Android Security Team's Classifications for Potentially
            Harmful Applications*, April 2016.
            https://static.googleusercontent.com/media/source.android.com/en//security/repor
            ts/Google_Android_Security_PHA_classifications.pdf

[18]   S. Frankel, B. Eydt, L Owens, K Scarefone, *Establishing Wireless Robust
            Security Networks: A Guide to IEEE 802.11i*, NIST, February 2007.
            http://nvlpubs.nist.gov/nistpubs/Legacy/SP/nistspecialpublication800-97.pdf

650

Appendix C— Mobile Threat Catalogue References

The following table contains references used to inform the Mobile Threat Catalogue.

[1]   N.O. Tippenhauer et al., "On the requirements for successful GPS spoofing attacks", in *Proceedings of the 18th ACM conference on Computer and communications security,* 2011, pp. 75-86; www.cs.ox.ac.uk/files/6489/gps.pdf [accessed 8/23/2016]

[2]   T.E. Humpreys et al. "Assessing the spoofing threat: Development of a portable GPS civilian spoofer." in *Proceedings of the 21st International Technical Meeting of the Satellite Division of The Institute of Navigation,* 2008, pp. 2314-2325; https://gps.mae.cornell.edu/humphreys_etal_iongnss2008.pdf [accessed 8/23/2016]

[3]   S. Andrivet, *The Security of MDM systems*, presented at Hack In Paris, 20 June 2013; https://hackinparis.com/data/slides/2013/MDM-HIP_2013.pdf [accessed 8/23/2016]

[4]   S. Breen, *Mobile Device Mismanagement*, presented at Blackhat, Aug. 2014; www.blackhat.com/docs/us-14/materials/us-14-Breen-Mobile-Device-Mismanagement.pdf [accessed 8/23/2016]

[5]   N.S. Evans, A. Benameur, and Y. Shen, "All Your Root Checks Are Belong to Us: The Sad State of Root Detection", in *Proceedings of the 13th ACM International Symposium on Mobility Management and Wireless Access,* 2015, pp. 81–88; http://dx.doi.org/10.1145/2810362.2810364 [accessed 8/23/2016]

[6]   D. Kravets, "Worker fired for disabling GPS app that track her 24 hours a day [Updated]", *Ars Technica*, 11 May 2015; http://arstechnica.com/tech-policy/2015/05/worker-fired-for-disabling-gps-app-that-tracked-her-24-hours-a-day/ [accessed 8/23/2016]

[7]   D. Denslow, "Personal Data Security and the "BYOD" Problem: Who is Truly at Risk?", blog, 19 Nov. 2014; http://jolt.richmond.edu/index.php/blog-personal-data-security-and-the-byod-problem-who-is-truly-at-risk/ [accessed 8/24/2016]

[8]   S. Raghuram, "Man in the Cloud: Threat, Impact, Resolution and the Bigger Picture", blog, 2015; www.skyhighnetworks.com/cloud-security-blog/man-in-the-cloud-threat-impact-resolution-and-the-bigger-picture/ [accessed 8/23/2016]

[9]   "Mobile Top 10 2016", Mar. 2016;
           www.owasp.org/index.php/Mobile_Top_10_2016-Top_10 [accessed
           8/23/2016]

[11]   L. Francis et al., "Practical NFC peer-to-peer relay attack using mobile
           phones", in *Proceedings of the 6th international conference on Radio
           frequency identification: security and privacy issues* (RFIDSec'10), 2010,
           pp. 35-49; https://eprint.iacr.org/2010/228.pdf [accessed 8/24/2016]

[12]   O. Cox, "Demystifying Point of Sale Malware and Attacks", blog, 25 Nov.
           2015; www.symantec.com/connect/blogs/demystifying-point-sale-malware-
           and-attacks [accessed 8/24/2016]

[13]   "Home Depot Hit By Same Malware as Target", 14 Sept. 2014;
           http://krebsonsecurity.com/2014/09/home-depot-hit-by-same-malware-as-
           target/ [accessed 8/24/2016]

[14]   M. Geuss, "The weak link in Apple Pay's strong chain is bank verification.
           Who's to blame?", *Ars Technica*, 3 Mar. 2015;
           http://arstechnica.com/apple/2015/03/the-weak-link-in-apple-pays-strong-
           chain-is-bank-verification-whos-to-blame/ [accessed 8/24/2016]

[15]   M. Georgiev et al., "The most dangerous code in the world: validating SSL
           certificates in non-browser software", in *Proceedings of the 2012 ACM
           conference on Computer and communications security* (CCS '12), 2012, pp.
           38-49; http://dx.doi.org/10.1145/2382196.2382204 [accessed 8/24/2016]

[16]   M. Souppaya and K. Scarfone, *Guidelines for Securing Wireless Local Area
           Networks (WLANs)*, SP 800-163, National Institute of Standards and
           Technology, 2016;
           http://nvlpubs.nist.gov/nistpubs/Legacy/SP/nistspecialpublication800-
           153.pdf [accessed 8/24/2016]

[17]   K. Zetter, "Darkhotel: A Sophisticated New Hacking Attack Targets High-
           Profile Hotel Guests", *Wired*, 10 Nov. 2014;
           www.wired.com/2014/11/darkhotel-malware/ [accessed 8/24/2016]

[18]   "CAPEC-613: WiFi SSID Tracking (Version 2.8)", MITRE, 7 Dec. 2015;
           http://capec.mitre.org/data/definitions/613.html [accessed 8/24/2016]

[19]   A. Stubblefield, J. Ioannidis and A.D. Rubin, *Using the Fluhrer, Mantin, and
           Shamir Attack to Break WEP*, tech. report TD-4ZCPZZ, AT&T Labs, 2001;
           www.isoc.org/isoc/conferences/ndss/02/papers/stubbl.pdf [accessed
           8/24/2016]

[20]   D. Richardson, "Using spoofed Wi-Fi to attack mobile devices", blog, 21 Apr. 2016; https://blog.lookout.com/blog/2016/04/21/spoofed-wi-fi-60-minutes/ [accessed 8/24/2016]

[21]   G. Fleishman, "FCC fines Marriott $600,000 for jamming hotel Wi-Fi", blog, 3 Oct. 2014; http://boingboing.net/2014/10/03/fcc-fines-marriott-for-jamming.html [accessed 8/24/2016]

[22]   B. Weis, *IEEE 802 Privacy Threat Analysis*, Cisco Systems, 2016; www.ieee802.org/1/files/public/docs2016/802E-weis-privacy-threat-analysis-0718-v01.pdf [accessed 8/24/2016]

[23]   B. Fung, "How stores use your phone's WiFi to track your shopping habits", *The Washington Post*, 19 Oct. 2013; www.washingtonpost.com/blogs/the-switch/wp/2013/10/19/how-stores-use-your-phones-wifi-to-track-your-shopping-habits [accessed 8/24/2016]

[24]   S. Clifford and Q. Hardy, "Attention, Shoppers: Store Is Tracking Your Cell", *The New York Times*, 14 July 2013; www.nytimes.com/2013/07/15/business/attention-shopper-stores-are-tracking-your-cell.html [accessed 8/24/2016]

[25]   S. Mlot, "FTC Goes After Firm for Tracking Shoppers' Cell Phones", PCMag, 24 Apr. 2015; www.pcmag.com/article2/0,2817,2482985,00.asp [accessed 8/24/2016]

[26]   "How Retailers Use Smartphones To Track Shoppers In The Store", *All Things Considered*, National Public Radio, 16 June 2014, transcript; www.npr.org/2014/06/16/322597862/how-retailers-use-smartphones-to-track-shoppers-in-the-store [accessed 8/24/2016]

[27]   *GPS, Wi-Fi, and Cell Phone Jammers Frequently Asked Questions (FAQs)*, Federal Communications Commission; https://transition.fcc.gov/eb/jammerenforcement/jamfaq.pdf [accessed 8/24/2016]

[28]   J. Padgette, K. Scarfone and L. Chen, *Guide to Bluetooth Security*, SP 800-121 rev. 1, National Institute of Standards and Technology, 2012; http://csrc.nist.gov/publications/nistpubs/800-121-rev1/sp800-121_rev1.pdf [accessed 8/24/2016]

[29]   C. Mulliner and M. Herfurt, "Blueprinting", 2013; http://trifinite.org/trifinite_stuff_blueprinting.html [accessed 8/24/2016]

[30]
         L. Carettoni, C. Merloni and S. Zanero, "Studying Bluetooth Malware

Propagation: The BlueBag Project", *Proceedings of the 2007 IEEE Symposium on Security and Privacy*, pp. 17-25, 2007; http://ieeexplore.ieee.org/stamp/stamp.jsp?arnumber=4140986 [accessed 8/24/2016]

[31]   Z. Wang et al., "Implementation and Analysis of a Practical NFC Relay Attack Example", in *Proceedings of the 2012 Second International Conference on Instrumentation, Measurement, Computer, Communication, and Control*, 2012, pp 143-146.

[32]   M. Maass et al., *Demo: NFCGate - An NFC Relay Application for Android [Extended Abstract]*, presented at 8th ACM Conference on Security and Privacy in Wireless and Mobile Networks, 26 June 2015; https://github.com/nfcgate/nfcgate [accessed 8/24/2016]

[33]   G. Vaughan, NFC Threat Landscape, OWASP Toronto chapter meeting, 31 Mar. 2013; www.owasp.org/images/3/38/NFC_Threat_Landscape_OWASP_Toronto_March_2013.pdf [accessed 8/24/2016]

[34]   C. Miller, *Exploring the NFC Attack Surface*, presented at Blackhat, 5 July 2012; https://media.blackhat.com/bh-us-12/Briefings/C_Miller/BH_US_12_Miller_NFC_attack_surface_WP.pdf [accessed 8/24/2016]

[35]   "Android 6.0 Changes", https://developer.android.com/about/versions/marshmallow/android-6.0-changes.html#behavior-hardware-id [accessed on 8/24/2016]

[36]   D. Stites and K. Skinner, *User Privacy on iOS and OS X,* presented at Apple Worldwide Developer Conference, June 2014; http://devstreaming.apple.com/videos/wwdc/2014/715xx4loqo5can9/715/715_user_privacy_in_ios_and_os_x.pdf [accessed 8/24/2016]

[37]   *Specification of the Bluetooth System version 1.0 B*, Bluetooth Special Interest Group, 1999; http://grouper.ieee.org/groups/802/15/Bluetooth/profile_10_b.pdf [accessed 8/24/2016]

[38]   "Security, Bluetooth Smart (Low Energy)", 2016; https://developer.bluetooth.org/TechnologyOverview/Pages/LE-Security.aspx [accessed 8/24/2016]

[39]   S. Cobb, "QR Codes and NFC Chips: Preview-and-authorize should be default", blog, 23 Apr. 2012; www.welivesecurity.com/2012/04/23/qr-codes-and-nfc-chips-preview-and-authorize-should-be-default/ [accessed

8/24/2016]

[40]   S. Lawson, "Ten Ways Your Smartphone Knows Where you Are",
          PCWorld, 6 Apr. 2012;
          www.pcworld.com/article/253354/ten_ways_your_smartphone_knows_wher
          e_you_are.html [accessed 8/25/2016]

[41]   J.S. Warner and R.G. Johnston, *GPS Spoofing Countermeasures*, tech. report
          LAUR-03-6163, Los Alamos National Laboratory, 2003;
          http://lewisperdue.com/DieByWire/GPS-Vulnerability-LosAlamos.pdf
          [accessed 8/25/2016]

[42]   "Malware Targeting Point of Sale Systems", US-CERT alert TA14-002A,
          US-CERT, 5 Feb. 2014; www.us-cert.gov/ncas/alerts/TA14-002A [accessed
          8/25/2016]

[43]   C. Xiao, "YiSpecter: First iOS Malware That Attacks Non-jailbroken Apple
          iOS Devices by Abusing Private APIs," blog, 25 Oct. 2015;
          http://researchcenter.paloaltonetworks.com/2015/10/yispecter-first-ios-
          malware-attacks-non-jailbroken-ios-devices-by-abusing-private-apis/

[44]   T. Claburn, "iOS SideStepper Vulnerability Undermines MDM Services:
          Check Point," *InformationWeek* ,31 Mar. 2016;
          www.informationweek.com/mobile/mobile-devices/ios-sidestepper-
          vulnerability-undermines-mdm-services-check-point/d/d-id/1324920

[45]   L. Tung, "Apple iPhone, iPad iOS 9 security flaw lets malicious apps sneak
          onto enterprise devices," *ZDNet*, 1 Apr. 2016; www.zdnet.com/article/apple-
          iphone-ipad-ios-9-security-flaw-lets-malicious-apps-sneak-onto-enterprise-
          devices/

[46]   B. Lau et al. , MACTANS: Injecting Malware Into iOS Devices Via
          Malicious Chargers, presented at BlackHat, 3-4 Aug. 2013.
          https://media.blackhat.com/us-13/US-13-Lau-Mactans-Injecting-Malware-
          into-iOS-Devices-via-Malicious-Chargers-WP.pdf [accessed 8/23/16].

[47]   M. Mendoza, "Xiaomi Locks Mi Devices' Bootloaders On Fears Of Malware
          And Security Risks: Up To 21 Days To Unlock," Tech Times, 20 Jan. 2016;
          www.techtimes.com/articles/125681/20160120/xiaomi-locks-mi-devices-
          bootloaders-on-fears-of-malware-and-security-risks-up-to21-days-to-
          unlock.htm [accessed 8/26/2016]

[48]   D. Pauli, "Samsung S6 calls open to man-in-the-middle base station
          snooping," *The Register*, 12 Nov. 2015;
          www.theregister.co.uk/2015/11/12/mobile_pwn2own1/

[49]   D. Goodin, "Software flaw puts mobile phones and networks at risk of
            complete takeover," *Ars Technica*, 19 July 2016;
            http://arstechnica.com/security/2016/07/software-flaw-puts-mobile-phones-
            and-networks-at-risk-of-complete-takeover/

[50]   R. Weinmann, Baseband Attacks: Remote Exploitation of Memory
            Corruptions in Cellular Protocol Stacks, presented at 6th USENIX
            Workshop on Offensive Technologies, 6-7 Aug. 2012;
            www.usenix.org/system/files/conference/woot12/woot12-final24.pdf
            [accessed 8/23/16].

[51]   G. Williams, "4 Surprising Ways Your Identity Can Be Stolen," *U.S. News
            & World Report*, 9 June 2015; http://money.usnews.com/money/personal-
            finance/articles/2015/06/09/4-surprising-ways-your-identity-can-be-stolen

[52]   "AT&T SIM-Card Switch Scam", New York Department of State;
            www.dos.ny.gov/consumerprotection/scams/att-sim.html [accessed 8/23/16].

[53]   R. Chirgwin, "This is what a root debug backdoor in a Linux kernel looks
            like," *The Register*, 9 May. 2016;
            www.theregister.co.uk/2016/05/09/allwinners_allloser_custom_kernel_has_
            a_nasty_root_backdoor/ [accessed 8/26/2016]

[54]   *iOS Security: iOS 9.3 or later, white paper, Apple, 2016.
            www.apple.com/business/docs/iOS_Security_Guide.pdf [accessed 8/24/16].*

[55]   R. Welton, "Remote Code Execution as System User on Samsung Phones",
            blog, 16 June 2015; www.nowsecure.com/blog/2015/06/16/remote-code-
            execution-as-system-user-on-samsung-phones/ [accessed 8/25/2016]

[56]   J. V. Dyke, "Insecurity Cameras and Mobile Apps: Surveillance or
            Exposure?", blog, 6 Jan. 2016;
            www.nowsecure.com/blog/2016/01/06/insecurity-cameras-and-mobile-apps-
            surveillance-or-exposure/ [accessed 8/25/2016]

[57]   J. Oberheide and Z. Lanier, "Team Joch vs. Android", presented at
            ShmooCon 2011, 28-30 Jan. 2011, slide 54;
            https://jon.oberheide.org/files/shmoo11-teamjoch.pdf [accessed 8/25/2016]

[61]   L. Neely, Mobile Threat Protection: A Holistic Approach to Securing
            Mobile Data and Devices, SANS Institute, 2016; www.sans.org/reading-
            room/whitepapers/analyst/mobile-threat-protection-holistic-approach-
            securing-mobile-data-devices-36715 [accessed 8/25/2016]

[62]
            S. Fahl et al, "Why Eve and Mallory Love Android: An Analysis of Android

SSL (In)Security", in *Proceedings of the 2012 ACM conference on Computer and Communications Security,* 2012, pp. 50-61; http://dl.acm.org/citation.cfm?id=2382205 [accessed 8/25/2016]

[63]   D. Sounthiraraj et al, "SMV-HUNTER: Large Scale, Automated Detection of SSL/TLS Man-in-the-Middle Vulnerabilities in Android Apps", in *Proceedings of the 2014 Network and Distributed System Security Symposium,* 2014; www.internetsociety.org/sites/default/files/10_3_1.pdf [accessed 8/25/2016]

[64]   A. Mettler et al, "SSL Vulnerabilities: Who Listens When Android Applications Talk?", 20 Aug. 2014; www.fireeye.com/blog/threat-research/2014/08/ssl-vulnerabilities-who-listens-when-android-applications-talk.html [accessed 8/25/2016]

[65]   J. Montelibano and W. Dormann, *How We Discovered Thousands of Vulnerable Android Apps in 1 Day,* presented at RSA Conference USA 2015, 19 Apr. 2015; www.rsaconference.com/writable/presentations/file_upload/hta-t08-how-we-discovered-thousands-of-vulnerable-android-apps-in-1-day_final.pdf [accessed 8/25/2016]

[66]   "Fandango, Credit Karma Settle FTC Charges that They Deceived Consumers By Failing to Securely Transmit Sensitive Personal Information", Federal Trade Commission, 28 Mar. 2014; www.ftc.gov/news-events/press-releases/2014/03/fandango-credit-karma-settle-ftc-charges-they-deceived-consumers [accessed 8/25/2016]

[67]   J. Case, "Exclusive: Vulnerability In Skype For Android Is Exposing Your Name, Phone Number, Chat Logs, And A Lot More", blog, 14 Apr. 2011; www.androidpolice.com/2011/04/14/exclusive-vulnerability-in-skype-for-android-is-exposing-your-name-phone-number-chat-logs-and-a-lot-more/# [accessed 8/25/2016]

[68]   J. V. Dyke, "World Writable Code Is Bad, MMMMKAY", blog, 10 Aug. 2015; www.nowsecure.com/blog/2015/08/10/world-writable-code-is-bad-mmmmkay/ [accessed 8/25/2016]

[69]   "[Vulnerability Identifier]: LOOK-11-001", blog, 1 Feb. 2011; https://blog.lookout.com/look-11-001/ [accessed 8/25/2016]

[70]   A. Donenfeld, *Stumping the Mobile Chipset,* presented at DEFCON 24, 7 Aug. 2016; https://media.defcon.org/DEF CON 24/DEF CON 24 presentations/DEFCON-24-Adam-Donenfeld-Stumping-The-Mobile-Chipset.pdf [accessed 8/25/2016]

[71]   A. Brandt, "Android Towelroot Exploit Used to Deliver Dogspectus Ransomware", blog, 25 Apr. 2016; www.bluecoat.com/security-blog/2016-04-25/android-exploit-delivers-dogspectus-ransomware [accessed 8/25/2016]

[72]   JailbreakMe; https://jailbreakme.qoid.us [accessed 8/25/2016]

[73]   R. Welton, "A Pattern for Remote Code Execution using Arbitrary File Writes and MultiDex Applications", blog, 15 June 2015; www.nowsecure.com/blog/2015/06/15/a-pattern-for-remote-code-execution-using-arbitrary-file-writes-and-multidex-applications/ [accessed 8/25/2016]

[74]   M. Grace et al, "Unsafe Exposure Analysis of Mobile In-App Advertisements", in *Proceedings of the Fifth ACM Conference on Security and Privacy in Wireless and Mobile Networks,*2012, pp. 101-112; http://dl.acm.org/citation.cfm?id=2185464 [accessed 8/25/2016]

[75]   S. Guerrero, "eBay for Android Content Provider Injection Vulnerability", blog, 4 Oct. 2013; www.nowsecure.com/blog/2013/10/04/ebay-for-android-content-provider-injection-vulnerability/ [accessed 8/25/2016]

[76]   X. Jiang, "Smishing Vulnerability in Multiple Android Platforms (including Gingerbread, Ice Cream Sandwich, and Jelly Bean)", 28 Nov. 2012; www.csc.ncsu.edu/faculty/jiang/smishing.html [accessed 8/25/2016]

[77]   T. Cannon, "Android SMS Spoofer", GitHub repository, 14 Dec. 2012; https://github.com/thomascannon/android-sms-spoof [accessed 8/25/2016]

[78]   K. Okuyama, "Content provider permission bypass allows malicious application to access data", Mozilla Foundation Security Advisory 2016-41, Mozilla Foundation, 26 Apr. 2016; www.mozilla.org/en-US/security/advisories/mfsa2016-41/ [accessed 8/25/2016]

[79]   "WebView addJavaScriptInterface Remote Code Execution", 24 Sept. 2013; https://labs.mwrinfosecurity.com/blog/webview-addjavascriptinterface-remote-code-execution/ [accessed 8/25/2016]

[80]   F. Long, "DRD13. Do not provide addJavascriptInterface method access in a WebView which could contain untrusted content. (API level JELLY_BEAN or below)", 8 Apr. 2015; www.securecoding.cert.org/confluence/pages/viewpage.action?pageId=129859614 [accessed 8/25/2016]

[81]   T. Sutcliffe, "Remote code execution on Android devices", blog, 31 July 2014; https://labs.bromium.com/2014/07/31/remote-code-execution-on-

android-devices/ [accessed 8/25/2016]

[82]   D. Andzakovic, *FortiClient Multiple Vulnerabilities*, vulnerability disclosure, 29 Jan. 2015; www.security-assessment.com/files/documents/advisory/Fortinet_FortiClient_Multiple_Vulnerabilities.pdf [accessed 8/25/2016]

[83]   *The Google Android Security Team's Classifications for Potentially Harmful Applications*, Apr. 2016; https://static.googleusercontent.com/media/source.android.com/en//security/reports/Google_Android_Security_PHA_classifications.pdf [accessed 8/25/2016]

[84]   W. Zhou et al., "Slembunk: An Evolving Android Trojan Family Targeting Users of Worldwide Banking Apps", blog, 17 Dec. 2015; www.fireeye.com/blog/threat-research/2015/12/slembunk_an_evolvin.html [accessed 8/25/2016]

[85]   Y. Zhou and X. Jiang, "Dissecting Android Malware: Characterization and Evolution", in *Proceedings of the 2012 IEEE Symposium on Security and Privacy*, 2012, pp 95-109; http://ieeexplore.ieee.org/document/6234407/?arnumber=6234407 [accessed 8/25/2016]

[86]   C. Zheng and Z. Xu, "New Android Malware Family Evades Antivirus Detection by Using Popular Ad Libraries", blog, 7 July 2015; http://researchcenter.paloaltonetworks.com/2015/07/new-android-malware-family-evades-antivirus-detection-by-using-popular-ad-libraries/ [accessed 8/25/2016]

[87]   "Unauthorized App Discovered", in Incident Response for Android and iOS, www.nowsecure.com/resources/mobile-incident-response/en/case-studies/unauthorized-app-discovered.html [accessed 8/25/2016]

[88]   M. Kelly, "Cloned banking app stealing usernames sneaks into Google Play", blog, 24 June 2014; https://blog.lookout.com/blog/2014/06/24/bankmirage/ [accessed 8/25/2016]

[89]   D. Richardson, "Change to sideloading apps in iOS 9 is a security win", blog, 10 Sept. 2015; https://blog.lookout.com/blog/2015/09/10/ios-9-sideloading/ [accessed 8/25/2016]

[90]   Mobile Security: Threats and Countermeasures, white paper, MobileIron; www.mobileiron.com/sites/default/files/security/Mobile-Security-Threats-and-Countermeasures-WP-MKT-6361-V1.pdf [accessed 8/25/2016]

[91]   D. Richardson, "Jailbreaking not a requirement for infecting iPhones with
          Hacking Team spyware", blog, 10 July 2015;
          https://blog.lookout.com/blog/2015/07/10/hacking-team/ [accessed
          8/25/2016]

[92]   L. Sun, et al, "Pawn Storm Update: iOS Espionage App Found", blog, 4 Feb.
          2015; http://blog.trendmicro.com/trendlabs-security-intelligence/pawn-
          storm-update-ios-espionage-app-found/ [accessed 8/25/2016]

[93]   C. Xiao, "WireLurker: A New Era in OS X and iOS Malware", blog, 5 Nov.
          2014; http://researchcenter.paloaltonetworks.com/2014/11/wirelurker-new-
          era-os-x-ios-malware/ [accessed 8/25/2016]

[94]   C. Page, "MKero: Android malware secretly subscribes victims to premium
          SMS services", *The Inquirer*, 9 Sept. 2015;
          www.theinquirer.net/inquirer/news/2425201/mkero-android-malware-
          secretly-subscribes-victims-to-premium-sms-services [accessed 8/25/2016]

[95]   T. Espiner, "Chinese Android botnet 'netting millions', says Symantec",
          ZDNet, 10 Feb. 2012; www.zdnet.com/article/chinese-android-botnet-
          netting-millions-says-symantec/ [accessed 8/25/2016]

[96]   C. Zheng, et al, "New Android Trojan XBot Phishes Credit Cards and Bank
          Accounts, Encrypts Devices for Ransom", blog, 18 Feb. 2016;
          http://researchcenter.paloaltonetworks.com/2016/02/new-android-trojan-
          xbot-phishes-credit-cards-and-bank-accounts-encrypts-devices-for-ransom/
          [accessed 8/25/2016]

[97]   R. K. Konoth, Victor van der Veen, and Herbert Bos, "How Anywhere
          Computing Just Killed Your Phone-Based Two-Factor Authentication",
          *Proceedings of the 20th Conference on Financial Cryptography and Data
          Security,* 2016; http://fc16.ifca.ai/preproceedings/24_Konoth.pdf [accessed
          8/25/2016]

[98]   *Android Security 2015 Year In Review*, Google, 2016;
          https://source.android.com/security/reports/Google_Android_Security_2015
          _Report_Final.pdf [accessed 8/25/2016]

[99]   D. Goodin, "Malware designed to take over cameras and record audio enters
          Google Play", *Ars Technica*, 7 Mar. 2014;
          http://arstechnica.com/security/2014/03/malware-designed-to-take-over-
          cameras-and-record-audio-enters-google-play/ [accessed 8/25/2016]

[100]   J. Oberheide, *Android Hax*, presented at Summercon, 10 June 2010;
          https://jon.oberheide.org/files/summercon10-androidhax-jonoberheide.pdf

[accessed 8/25/2016]

[101]   P. Ducklin, "How to clean up the Duh iPhone worm", *Naked Security*, Sophos, 24 Nov. 2009; https://nakedsecurity.sophos.com/2009/11/24/clean-up-iPhone-worm/ [accessed 8/25/2016]

[102]   C. Dehghanpoor, "Brain Test re-emerges: 13 apps found in Google Play", blog, 6 Jan. 2016; https://blog.lookout.com/blog/2016/01/06/brain-test-re-emerges/ [accessed 8/25/2016]

[103]   V. Chebyshev and R. Unuchek, "Mobile Malware Evolution: 2013", blog, 24 Feb. 2014; https://securelist.com/analysis/kaspersky-security-bulletin/58335/mobile-malware-evolution-2013/ [accessed 8/25/2016]

[104]   A. Coletta et al, "DroydSeuss: A Mobile Banking Trojan Tracker – A Short Paper", in *Proceedings of Financial Cryptography and Data Security 2016*, 2016; http://fc16.ifca.ai/preproceedings/14_Coletta.pdf [accessed 8/25/2016]

[105]   A.P. Felt and D. Wagner, *Phishing on Mobile Devices*, presented at Web 2.0 Security & Privacy 2011, 26 May 2011; http://w2spconf.com/2011/papers/felt-mobilephishing.pdf [accessed 8/25/2016]

[106]   R. Hassell, *Exploiting Androids for Fun and Profit,* presented at Hack In The Box Security Conference 2011, 12-13 Oct. 2011; http://conference.hitb.org/hitbsecconf2011kul/materials/D1T1 - Riley Hassell - Exploiting Androids for Fun and Profit.pdf [accessed 8/25/2016]

[107]   W. Zhou et al., "The Latest Android Overlay Malware Spreading via SMS Phishing in Europe", blog, 28 June 2016; www.fireeye.com/blog/threat-research/2016/06/latest-android-overlay-malware-spreading-in-europe.html [accessed 8/25/2016]

[108]   J. Clover, "Password-Stealing Instagram App 'InstaAgent' Reappears in App Store Under New Name", *MacRumors*, 22 Mar. 2016; www.macrumors.com/2016/03/22/password-stealing-instaagent-app-reappears/ [accessed 8/25/2016]

[109]   T. Fox-Brewster, "Hackers Sneak Malware Into Apple App Store 'To Steal iCloud Passwords'", *Forbes*, 18 Sept. 2015; www.forbes.com/sites/thomasbrewster/2015/09/18/xcodeghost-malware-wants-your-icloud/ [accessed 8/25/2016]

[110]   *Internet Security Threat Report vol. 21*, Symantec, 2016.

NISTIR 8144 (DRAFT)   ASSESSING THREATS TO MOBILE TECHNOLOGIES

[111]   T. Wang et al., "Jekyll on iOS: When Benign Apps Become Evil", in *Proceedings of the 22nd USENIX Security Symposium*, 2013; www.usenix.org/system/files/conference/usenixsecurity13/sec13-paper_wang_2.pdf [accessed 8/25/2016]

[112]   D. Storm, "Mobile RAT attack makes Android the ultimate spy tool", *Computerworld*, 1 Mar. 2012; www.computerworld.com/article/2472441/cybercrime-hacking/mobile-rat-attack-makes-android-the-ultimate-spy-tool.html [accessed 8/25/2016]

[113]   L. Fair, "Device Squad: The story behind the FTC's first case against a mobile device maker", blog, 22 Feb. 2013; www.ftc.gov/news-events/blogs/business-blog/2013/02/device-squad-story-behind-ftcs-first-case-against-mobile [accessed 8/25/2016]

[114]   Check Point Security Team, "Certifi-gate: Hundreds of Millions of Android Devices Could Be Pwned", blog, 6 Aug. 2015; http://blog.checkpoint.com/2015/08/06/certifigate/ [accessed 8/25/2016]

[115]   "Samsung Keyboard Security Risk Disclosed", 16 June 2015; www.nowsecure.com/keyboard-vulnerability/ [accessed 8/25/2016]

[116]   *CBS App & Mobility Website*, Wandera Threat Advisory No. 192, Wandera, 23 Mar. 2016; www.wandera.com/resources/dl/TA_CBS.pdf [accessed 8/24/2016]

[117]   *The Fork*, Wandera Threat Advisory No. 154, Wandera, 14 Jan. 2016; www.wandera.com/resources/dl/TA_The_Fork.pdf [accessed 8/24/2016]

[118]   *Star Q8*, Wandera Threat Advisory No. 152, Wandera, 10 Jan. 2016; www.wandera.com/resources/dl/TA_StarQ8.pdf [accessed 8/24/2016]

[119]   Corriere Della Sera App, Wandera Threat Advisory No. 74, Wandera, 29 Aug. 2015; www.wandera.com/resources/dl/TA_CorriereDellaSeraApp.pdf (accessed 24 Aug 2016)

[120]   *La Tribune*, Wandera Threat Advisory No. 84, Wandera, 2 Oct. 2015; www.wandera.com/resources/dl/TA_LaTribune.pdf [accessed 8/24/2016]

[121]   *Card Crypt*, Wandera Threat Advisory No. 142, Wandera, 9 Dec. 2015; www.wandera.com/resources/dl/TA_CardCrypt.pdf [accessed 8/24/2016]

[122]   E. Schuman, "Starbucks Caught Storing Mobile Passwords in Clear Text", *Computerworld*, 15 Jan. 2014; www.computerworld.com/article/2487743/security0/evan-schuman--

starbucks-caught-storing-mobile-passwords-in-clear-text.html [accessed 8/25/2016]

[124]   A. Aviv et al., "Smudge Attacks on Smartphone Touch Screens", in *Proceedings of the 4th USENIX Conference on Offensive technologies*, 2010; www.usenix.org/legacy/event/woot10/tech/full_papers/Aviv.pdf [accessed 8/24/2016].

[125]   P. Ducklin, "Black Box" Brouhaha Breaks Out Over Brute Forcing of iPhone Pin Lock", *Naked Security*, Sophos, 17 Mar. 2015; https://nakedsecurity.sophos.com/2015/03/17/black-box-brouhaha-breaks-out-over-brute-forcing-of-iphone-pin-lock/ [accessed 8/25/2016]

[126]   T. Simonite, "Black Hat: Google Glass Can Steal Your Passcodes", *MIT Technology Review*, 7 Aug. 2014; www.technologyreview.com/s/529896/black-hat-google-glass-can-steal-your-passcodes/ [accessed 8/25/2016]

[127]   L. Tung, "iOS 9 LockScreen Bypass Exposes Photos and Contacts", *ZDNet*, 24 Sept. 2015; www.zdnet.com/article/ios-9-lockscreen-bypass-exposes-photos-and-contacts/ [accessed 8/25/2016]

[128]   S. Hill, "Your Smartphone Isn't As Safe As You'd Think, Techradar, 29 Nov. 2013; www.techradar.com/us/news/phone-and-communications/mobile-phones/your-smartphone-pin-isn-t-as-safe-as-you-d-think-1203510 [accessed 8/25/2016]

[129]   D. Goodin, "How hackers can access iPhone contacts and photos without a password", *Ars Technica*, 25 Sept. 2015; http://arstechnica.com/security/2015/09/how-hackers-can-access-iphone-contacts-and-photos-without-a-password/ [accessed 8/25/2016]

[130]   D. Goodin, "Serious OS X and iOS Flaws Let Hackers Steal Keychain, 1Password Contents", *Ars Technica*, 17 June 2015; http://arstechnica.com/security/2015/06/serious-os-x-and-ios-flaws-let-hackers-steal-keychain-1password-contents/ [accessed 8/25/2016]

[131]   J. Lemonnier, "Which is the most secure Android Smart Lock?", 4 June 2016; http://now.avg.com/which-is-the-most-secure-android-smart-lock/ [accessed 8/25/2016]

[132]   J. Trader, "Liveness Detection to Fight Biometric Spoofing", blog, 22 July 2014; http://blog.m2sys.com/scanning-and-efficiency/liveness-detection-fight-biometric-spoofing/ [accessed 8/25/2016]

[133]   M. Rogers "Why I hacked TouchID (again) and still think it's awesome", blog, 23 Sept. 2016; https://blog.lookout.com/blog/2014/09/23/iphone-6-touchid-hack; [accessed 8/25/2016]

[134]   D. Richardson, "Using Spoofed Wi-Fi to Attack Mobile Devices", blog, 21 Apr. 2016; https://blog.lookout.com/blog/2016/04/21/spoofed-wi-fi-60-minutes/ [accessed 8/25/2016]

[135]   SRLabs, "iPhone 5S Touch ID susceptible to fingerprint spoofs", YouTube video, 25 Sept. 2013; www.youtube.com/watch?v=h1n_tS9zxMc [accessed 8/25/2016]; Note, URL https://srlabs.de/spoofing-fingerprints/ - not available

[136]   "Man-in-the-Middle Attack", 31 Aug. 2015; www.owasp.org/index.php/Man-in-the-middle_attack [accessed 8/25/2016]

[138]   R. Graves, Phishing Defenses for Webmail Providers, white paper, SANS Institute, 2013; www.sans.org/reading-room/whitepapers/email/phishing-detecton-remediation-34082 [accessed 8/258/2016]

[139]   C. Boyd, "'Your Account PayPal Has Been Limited' Phishing Scam", blog, 8 May 2015; https://blog.malwarebytes.com/cybercrime/2015/05/your-account-paypal-has-been-limited-phishing-scam/ [accessed 8/25/2016]

[140]   A. Wulf, "Stealing Passwords is Easy in Native Mobile Apps Despite OAuth", blog, 12 Jan. 2011; http://welcome.totheinter.net/2011/01/12/stealing-passwords-is-easy-in-native-mobile-apps-despite-oauth/ [accessed 8/25/2016]

[141]   W. Denniss and J. Bradley, "OAuth 2.0 for Native Apps", IETF Internet Draft, work in progress, July 2016.

[142]   J.F. Miller, "Supply Chain Attack Framework and Attack Patterns", tech. report, MITRE, Dec. 2013; www.mitre.org/sites/default/files/publications/supply-chain-attack-framework-14-0228.pdf

[143]   Z. Wang and A. Stavrou, "Exploiting Smart-Phone USB Connectivity for Fun and Profit", in *Proceedings of 26th Annual Computer Security Applications Conference,* 2010, pp. 357-365

[144]   A. Stavrou, Z. Wang, *Exploiting Smart-Phone USB Connectivity For Fun And Profit*, presented at Blackhat, 4 Aug. 2011; https://media.blackhat.com/bh-dc-11/Stavrou-Wang/BlackHat_DC_2011_Stavrou_Zhaohui_USB_exploits-Slides.pdf

[accessed 8/25/2016]

[145]   M. Brignall, "Sim-Swap Fraud Claims Another Mobile Banking Victim",
            The Guardian, 16 Apr. 2016;
            www.theguardian.com/money/2016/apr/16/sim-swap-fraud-mobile-banking-
            fraudsters [accessed 8/25/2016]

[146]   *BYOD & Mobile Security*, Information Security Community on LinkedIn,
            Apr. 2016;
            http://get.skycure.com/hubfs/Reports/BYOD_and_Mobile_Security_Report_
            2016.pdf [accessed 8/25/2016]

[147]   V. Blue, "Researchers Show How to Hack an iPhone in 60 Seconds",
            ZDNet, 31 July 2013; www.zdnet.com/article/researchers-reveal-how-to-
            hack-an-iphone-in-60-seconds/ [accessed 8/25/2016]

[149]   A. O'Donnell, "How to Protect Yourself From Malicious QR Codes", blog,
            http://netsecurity.about.com/od/securityadvisorie1/a/How-To-Protect-
            Yourself-From-Malicious-QR-Codes.htm [accessed 8/25/16].

[150]   G. Gruman, "Keep out hijackers: Secure your app store dev account,"
            InfoWorld, 5 Dec. 2014; www.infoworld.com/article/2854963/mobile-
            development/how-to-keep-your-app-store-dev-account-from-being-
            hijacked.html

[151]   D. Fisher, "Researchers Find Methods for Bypassing Google's Bouncer
            Android Security," blog, 4 June 2012; https://threatpost.com/researchers-
            find-methods-bypassing-googles-bouncer-android-security-060412/76643/

[152]   C. Welch, "Major security hole allows Apple passwords to be reset with
            only email address, date of birth (update)," *The Verge*, 22 Mar. 2013;
            www.theverge.com/2013/3/22/4136242/major-security-hole-allows-apple-
            id-passwords-reset-with-email-date-of-birth

[153]   D. Harkness et al., "Google Play Store seems blocked now from China. How
            can I update my Quora app?", forum thread, 6 Dec. 2014,
            www.quora.com/Google-Play-Store-seems-blocked-now-from-China-How-
            can-I-update-my-Quora-app [accessed 8/25/16].

[154]   J. Cheng, "'Find and Call' app becomes first trojan to appear on iOS App
            Store," *Ars Technica*, 5 July 2012;
            http://arstechnica.com/apple/2012/07/find-and-call-app-becomes-first-trojan-
            to-appear-on-ios-app-store/

[155]   J. Miller and C. Oberheide, *Dissecting the Android Bouncer,* Summercon,

June 2012. https://jon.oberheide.org/files/summercon12-bouncer.pdf [accessed 8/25/16].

[156]   N.J. Percoco and S. Schulte, *Adventures in BouncerLand*, presented at BlackHat, 25 July 2012. https://media.blackhat.com/bh-us-12/Briefings/Percoco/BH_US_12_Percoco_Adventures_in_Bouncerland_W P.pdf [accessed 8/25/16].

[158]   "Setup an FDroid App Repo", wiki entry, 3 May 2016, https://f-droid.org/wiki/page/Setup_an_FDroid_App_Repo [accessed 8/25/16].

[159]   "Protect your developer account" , Google, 2016, https://support.google.com/googleplay/android-developer/answer/2543765?hl=en [accessed 8/25/16].

[160]   "Security and your Apple ID", Apple, 2016, https://support.apple.com/en-us/HT201303 [accessed 8/25/16].

[161]   "Maintaining Your Signing Identities and Certificates", Apple, 5 July 2016, https://developer.apple.com/library/prerelease/content/documentation/IDEs/Conceptual/AppDistributionGuide/MaintainingCertificates/MaintainingCertificates.html [accessed 8/25/16].

[162]   "Secure Your Private Key", in *User Guide,* https://developer.android.com/studio/publish/app-signing.html#secure-key [accessed 8/25/16].

[164]   D. Goodin, "New Attack Steals Secret Crypto Keys from Android and iOS Phones", *Ars Technica*, 3 Mar. 2016; http://arstechnica.com/security/2016/03/new-attack-steals-secret-crypto-keys-from-android-and-ios-phones/ [accessed 8/25/2016]

[165]   *3G Security; Security Threats and Requirements (Release 4)*, 3GPP TS 21.133 V4.0.0, 3rd Generation Partnership Project, 2003; www.3gpp.org/ftp/tsg_sa/wg3_security/_specs/Old_Vsns/21133-400.pdf [Accessed 8/23/2016]

[166]   J. Cichonski, J.M. Franklin, and M. Bartock, LTE Architecture Overview and Security Analysis, Draft NISTIR 8071, National Institute of Standards and Technology, 2016; http://csrc.nist.gov/publications/drafts/nistir-8071/nistir_8071_draft.pdf [Accessed 8/23/2016]

[167]   R.P. Jover, *LTE Security and Protocol Exploits*, presented at ShmooCon, 3 Jan. 2016; www.ee.columbia.edu/~roger/ShmooCon_talk_final_01162016.pdf

[accessed 8/23/2016]

[168]   J. Vijayan, "Researchers Exploit Cellular Tech Flaws to Intercept Phone
          Calls", *ComputerWorld*, 1 Aug. 2013;
          http://www.computerworld.com/article/2484538/cybercrime-
          hacking/researchers-exploit-cellular-tech-flaws-to-intercept-phone-calls.html
          [accessed 8/23/2016]

[169]   J. Kakar et al. "Analysis and Mitigation of Interference to the LTE Physical
          Control Format Indicator Channel", in *Proceedings of 2014 IEEE Military
          Communications Conference*, 2014, pp. 228-234.

[170]   C.-Y. Li et al. "Insecurity of Voice Solution VoLTE in LTE Mobile
          Networks", In *Proceedings of the 22nd ACM SIGSAC Conference on
          Computer and Communications Security (CCS '15)*, 2015, pp. 316-327;
          http://dx.doi.org/10.1145/2810103.2813618 [accessed 8/23/2016]

[171]   *Safe Use of Mobile Devices and the Internet*, CESG, 2016;
          www.cesg.gov.uk/guidance/safe-use-mobile-devices-and-internet [accessed
          8/23/2016]

[172]   P. Langlois, *SCTPscan - Finding Entry Points to SS7 Networks &
          Telecommunication Backbones*, presented at Blackhat EU, 29 Mar. 2007;
          www.blackhat.com/presentations/bh-europe-07/Langlois/Presentation/bh-eu-
          07-langlois-ppt-apr19.pdf [accessed 8/23/2016]

[173]   K. Nohl, *GSM Sniffing*, 27th Chaos Communication Congress, Dec. 2010;
          https://events.ccc.de/congress/2010/Fahrplan/attachments/1783_101228.27C
          3.GSM-Sniffing.Nohl_Munaut.pdf [accessed 8/23/2016]

[174]   P. Langlois, *Toward the HLR: Attacking the SS7 & SIGTRAN Applications*,
          presented at H2HC, Dec. 2009;
          www.h2hc.org.br/repositorio/2009/files/Philippe.en.pdf [accessed
          8/23/2016]

[175]   K. Nohl, *Attacking Phone Privacy*, presented at Blackhat, 29 July 2010;
          https://media.blackhat.com/bh-ad-10/Nohl/BlackHat-AD-2010-Nohl-
          Attacking-Phone-Privacy-wp.pdf [accessed 8/23/2016]

[176]   U. Meyer and S. Wetzel, "A Man-in-the-Middle Attack on UMTS",
          Proceedings of the 3rd ACM workshop on Wireless security, 2004, pp. 90-
          97; http://dx.doi.org/10.1145/1023646.1023662 [accessed 8/23/2016]

[177]   H. Schmidt and B. Butterly, *Attacking BaseStations - an Odyssey through a
          Telco's Network*, presented at DEFCON 24, 7 Aug. 2016;

https://media.defcon.org/DEF CON 24/DEF CON 24
presentations/DEFCON-24-Hendrik-Schmidt-Brian-Butter-Attacking-
BaseStations.pdf [accessed 8/23/2016]

[178]   C. Feest, *Protecting Mobile Networks from SS7 Attacks*, white paper,
           Telesoft Technologies Inc., 2015; http://telesoft-
           technologies.com/document-library/milborne-ss7-firewall-ips/12-telesoft-
           whitepaper-protecting-mobile-networks-from-ss7-attacks/file [accessed
           8/23/2016]

[179]   H. Hu and N. Wei, "A Study of GPS Jamming and Anti-Jamming", in
           *Proceedings of Power Electronics and Intelligent Transportation System
           (PEITS), 2009 2nd International Conference on*, 2009, pp. 388-391.

[180]   D. DePerry and T. Ritter, *I Can Hear You Now: Traffic Interception and
           Remote Mobile Phone Cloning with a Compromised CDMA Femtocell*,
           presented at DEFCON 21, 2 Aug. 2013; www.defcon.org/images/defcon-
           21/dc-21-presentations/DePerry-Ritter/DEFCON-21-DePerry-Ritter-
           Femtocell-Updated.pdf [accessed 8/29/2016]

[181]   G.-H. Tu et al., "How Voice Call Technology Poses Security Threats in 4G
           LTE Networks", in *Proceedings of 2015 IEEE Conference on
           Communications and Network Security (CNS)*, 2015.

[182]   Z. Lackey, *Attacking SMS*, presented at Blackhat, 30 July 2009;
           www.blackhat.com/presentations/bh-usa-09/LACKEY/BHUSA09-Lackey-
           AttackingSMS-SLIDES.pdf [accessed 8/29/2016]

[183]   D. Goodin, "Beware of the Text Massage That Crashes iPhones", *Ars
           Technica*, 27 May 2015; http://arstechnica.com/security/2015/05/beware-of-
           the-text-message-that-crashes-iphones/ [accessed 8/29/2016]

[184]   P. Traynor et al., "Mitigating Attacks on Open Functionality in SMS-
           Capable Cellular Networks", in *IEEE/ACM Transaction on Networking 17.1*,
           2009; http://www.cc.gatech.edu/~traynor/papers/mobicom06.pdf [accessed
           8/29/2016]

[185]   N.J. Croft and M.S. Olivier, "A Silent SMS Denial of Servie (DoS) Attack",
           in *Information and Computer Security Architectures (ICSA) Research Group
           South Africa*, 2007; http://mo.co.za/open/silentdos.pdf [accessed 8/29/2016]

[186]   Z. Avraham, J. Drake, and N. Bassen, "Zimperium zLabs is Raising the
           Volume: New Vulnerability Processing MP3/MP4 Media", blog, 1 Oct.
           2015; https://blog.zimperium.com/zimperium-zlabs-is-raising-the-volume-
           new-vulnerability-processing-mp3mp4-media/ [accessed 8/29/2016]

[187]   M. Smith, "'Dirty USSD' Code Could Automatically Wipe Your Samsung
         TouchWize Device (Updated)", *Engadget,* 25 Oct. 2012;
         https://www.engadget.com/2012/09/25/dirty-ussd-code-samsung-hack-wipe/
         [accessed 8/29/2016]

[188]   "Remote USSD Code Execution on Android Devices", 29 Oct. 2012,
         https://www.nowsecure.com/blog/2012/09/25/remote-ussd-code-execution-
         on-android-devices/ [accessed 8/29/2016]

[189]   K. Nohn, *Mobile Self-Defense*, presented at 31st Chaos Communication
         Congress, 27 Dec. 2014;
         https://events.ccc.de/congress/2014/Fahrplan/system/attachments/2493/origi
         nal/Mobile_Self_Defense-Karsten_Nohl-31C3-v1.pdf [accessed 8/29/2016]

[190]   "New VMSA-2014-0014 – AirWatch by VMWare Product Update
         Addresses Information Disclosure Vulnerabilities", 10 Dec. 2014;
         http://seclists.org/fulldisclosure/2014/Dec/44 [accessed 8/29/2016]

[191]   G. Lorenz et al., "Securing SS7 Telecommunications Networks",
         in *Workshop on Information Assurance and Security vol. 2*, 2001.

[192]   C. Xiao, "BackStab: Mobile Backup Data Under Attack from Malware",
         paloalto, 7 Dec. 2015;
         http://researchcenter.paloaltonetworks.com/2015/12/backstab-mobile-
         backup-data-under-attack-from-malware/ [accessed 8/29/2016]

[193]   "BackStab: Mobile Backup Data Under Attack From Malware", 7 Dec.
         2015; https://www.paloaltonetworks.com/resources/research/unit42-
         backstab-mobile-backup-data-under-attack-from-malware.html [accessed
         8/29/2016]

[194]   "Elcomsoft Phone Breaker"; https://www.elcomsoft.com/eppb.html
         [accessed 8/29/2016]

[195]   Q4 Mobile Security and Risk Review, white paper, MobileIron;
         https://www.mobileiron.com/sites/default/files/qsreports/files/security-
         report-Q415-v1.2-EN.pdf [accessed 8/25/2016]

[196]   Security Guidance for Critical Areas of Mobile Computing, white paper,
         Cloud Security Alliance;
         https://downloads.cloudsecurityalliance.org/initiatives/mobile/Mobile_Guida
         nce_v1.pdf [accessed 8/29/2016]

[197]   M. Honan, "How Apple Aan Amazon Security Flaws Led To My Epic
         Hacking", *Wired*, 6 Aug. 2012; http://www.wired.com/2012/08/apple-

amazon-mat-honan-hacking/ [accessed 8/24/2016]

[198]   B. Thompson, "UAE Blackberry update was spyware", 21 Jul. 2009, http://news.bbc.co.uk/2/hi/8161190.stm [accessed 8/29/2016]

[199]   Appthority, "The State of the Mobile Ecosystem, Appthority Unveils New Security Research at Black Hat", 4 Aug. 2015, https://www.appthority.com/company/news-and-events/press-releases/the-state-of-the-mobile-ecosystem-appthority-unveils-new-security-research-at-black-hat/ [accessed 8/29/2015]

[200]   J. Oberheide, "How I Almost Won Pwn2Own via XSS", 07 Mar. 2011; https://jon.oberheide.org/blog/2011/03/07/how-i-almost-won-pwn2own-via-xss/ [accessed 8/25/2016]

[201]   R. Konoth, V. van der Veen et al., "How Anywhere Computing Just Killed Your Phone-Based Two-Factor Authentication", in Proceedings of the *20th Conference on Financial Cryptography and Data Security*, 2016

[202]   J. Forristal, *Android: One Root to Own Them All*, presented at Blackhat, 2013; https://media.blackhat.com/us-13/US-13-Forristal-Android-One-Root-to-Own-Them-All-Slides.pdf [accessed 8/24/2016]

[203]   J. Timmer, "UAE cellular carrier rolls out spyware as a 3G 'update'", *Ars Technica*, 23 Jul 2009; http://arstechnica.com/business/2009/07/mobile-carrier-rolls-out-spyware-as-a-3g-update/ [accessed 8/23/2016]

[204]   "Government Mobile and Wireless Security Baseline", CIO Council, 23 May 2013

[205]   Y. Amit, "Malicious Profiles – The Sleeping Giant of iOS Security", *Skycure Blog*, 12 Mar. 2013; https://www.skycure.com/blog/malicious-profiles-the-sleeping-giant-of-ios-security/ [accessed 8/23/2016]

[206]   "Android Security Bulletin—June 2016", 8 Dec. 2016; http://source.android.com/security/bulletin/2016-06-01.html [accessed 8/29/2016]

[207]   R. Chirgwin, "This is what a root debug backdoor in a Linux kernel looks like," *The Register*, 9 May. 2016; http://www.theregister.co.uk/2016/05/09/allwinners_allloser_custom_kernel_has_a_nasty_root_backdoor/

[208]   S. Gallagher, "Chinese ARM vendor left developer backdoor in kernel for Android, other devices," *Ars Technica*, 11 May 2016;

http://arstechnica.com/security/2016/05/chinese-arm-vendor-left-developer-backdoor-in-kernel-for-android-pi-devices/

[209]   laginimaineb, "Extracting Qualcomm's KeyMaster Keys - Breaking Android Full Disk Encryption," blog, 30 Jun. 2016; https://bits-please.blogspot.com/2016/06/extracting-qualcomms-keymaster-keys.html

[210]   ARM Security Technology Building a Secure System using TrustZone Technology; http://infocenter.arm.com/help/index.jsp?topic=/com.arm.doc.prd29-genc-009492c/ch01s03s03.html [accessed 8/23/16].

[211]   The SRLabs Team, *Rooting SIM cards*, presented at BlackHat, 2013. https://media.blackhat.com/us-13/us-13-Nohl-Rooting-SIM-cards-Slides.pdf [accessed 8/23/16].

[212]   H. Ko and R. Caytiles, "A Review of Smartcard Security Issues," Journal of Security Engineering, 8, no. 3 (2011): 6. http://www.sersc.org/journals/JSE/vol8_no3_2011/3.pdf [accessed 8/23/16].

[213]   zLabs, "Zimperium Applauds Google's Rapid Response to Unpatched Kernel Exploit," Zimperium, 25 Mar. 2016; https://blog.zimperium.com/zimperium-applauds-googles-rapid-response-to-unpatched-kernel-exploit/

[214]   W. Xu and Y. Fu, Own your Android! Yet Another Universal Root, presented at BlackHat, 2015. https://www.blackhat.com/docs/us-15/materials/us-15-Xu-Ah-Universal-Android-Rooting-Is-Back-wp.pdf [accessed 8/23/16].

[215]   TALOS Vulnerability Report; http://www.talosintelligence.com/reports/TALOS-2016-0186/ [accessed 8/23/16].

[216]   windknown, "iOS 8.4.1 Kernel Vulnerabilities in AppleHDQGasGaugeControl," Pangu, 08 Sept. 2015; http://blog.pangu.io/ios-8-4-1-kernel-vulns/

[217]   B. Lau et. al. , Injecting Malware into iOS Devices via Maliscious Chargers, presented at BlackHat, 2013. https://media.blackhat.com/us-13/US-13-Lau-Mactans-Injecting-Malware-into-iOS-Devices-via-Malicious-Chargers-WP.pdf [accessed 8/23/16].

[218]   Threat Advisory Semi Jailbreak; https://www.wandera.com/resources/dl/TA_SemiJailbreak.pdf [accessed

8/23/16].

[219]   A. Chaykin, "Spoofing and intercepting SIM commands through STK
             framework," blog, 26 Aug. 2015; http://blog.0xb.in/2015/08/spoofing-and-
             intercepting-sim-commands.html

[220]   "Security Enhancements in Android 4.3";
             https://source.android.com/security/enhancements/enhancements43.html
             [accessed 8/29/2016]

[221]   "Security Enhancements in Android 6.0";
             https://source.android.com/security/enhancements/enhancements60.html
             [accessed 8/29/2016]

[222]   "Trusty TEE"; https://source.android.com/security/trusty/index.html#third-
             party_trusty_applications [accessed 8/29/2016]

[223]   B. Krebs, "Beware of Juice-Jacking", 11 Aug. 2011;
             http://krebsonsecurity.com/2011/08/beware-of-juice-jacking/ [accessed
             8/24/2016]

[224]   P. Paganini, "Hacking Samsung Galaxy via Modem interface exposed via
             USB", 13 Apr. 2016;
             http://securityaffairs.co/wordpress/46287/hacking/hacking-samsung-
             galaxy.html [accessed 8/24/2016]

[225]   "Phone Theft in America: What really happens when your phone gets
             grabbed", blog, 7 May 2014;
             https://blog.lookout.com/blog/2014/05/07/phone-theft-in-america/ [accessed
             8/25/2016]

[226]   C. Deitrick, "Smartphone thefts drop as kill switch usage grows", Consumer
             Reports, 11 Jun 2015;
             http://www.consumerreports.org/cro/news/2015/06/smartphone-thefts-on-
             the-decline/index.htm [accessed 8/30/2016]

[227]   "Security Tips", https://developer.android.com/training/articles/security-
             tips.html [accessed on 8/24/2016]

[228]   "GenericKeychain",
             https://developer.apple.com/library/ios/samplecode/GenericKeychain/Introd
             uction/Intro.html#//apple_ref/doc/uid/DTS40007797 [accessed 8/25/16]

[229]   D. Genkin et al., ECDSA Key Extraction from Mobile Devices Via
             Nonintrusive Physical Side Channels, tech. report 2016/230, Cryptology

ePrint Archive, 2016; https://www.tau.ac.il/~tromer/mobilesc/mobilesc.pdf [accessed 8/31/2016]

[230]   "FAQ on Lost/Stolen Devices", in *Your Wireless Life*, July 2016; http://www.ctia.org/your-wireless-life/consumer-tips/how-to-deter-smartphone-thefts-and-protect-your-data/faq-on-lost-stolen-devices#anti-theft-commitment [accessed 8/31/2016]

[231]   "Eight Ways to Keep Your Smartphone Safe", in *BullGuard Security Centre*; www.bullguard.com/bullguard-security-center/mobile-security/mobile-protection-resources/8-ways-to-keep-your-smartphone-safe.aspx [accessed 8/31/2016]

[232]   G. Sims, "New Malware Tries to Infect Android Devices Via USB Cable", 27 Jan. 2014; www.androidauthority.com/new-malware-tries-infect-android-devices-via-usb-cable-339356/ [accessed 8/31/2016]

[233]   P. Warren, "Who's Got Your Old Phone's Data?", *The Guardian*, 23 Sept. 2008; www.theguardian.com/technology/2008/sep/25/news.mobilephones [accessed 8/31/2016]

[234]   *The Current State of Android Security*, infographic, Duo Labs, Jan 2016; https://duo.com/assets/infographics/The State of Android Security 72.png [accessed 8/31/2016]

[235]   L. Jordaan and B. von Solms, "A Biometrics-Based Solution to Combat SIM Swap Fraud", in *Open Research Problems in Network Security*, pp. 70-87, 2011

[236]   Juniper Networks Third Annual Mobile Threats Report, white paper, Juniper Networks; http://www.juniper.net/us/en/local/pdf/additional-resources/jnpr-2012-mobile-threats-report.pdf [accessed 8/31/16]

[237]   M. Rogers, "Dendroid malware can take over your camera, record audio, and sneak into Google Play", blog, 6 Mar. 2014;https://blog.lookout.com/blog/2014/03/06/dendroid/ [accessed 8/31/16]

[238]   X. Zhang and W. Du, "Attacks on Android Clipboard", Detection of Intrusions and Malware and Vulnerability Assessment: 11th International Conference, 2014;http://www.cis.syr.edu/~wedu/Research/paper/clipboard_attack_dimva 2014.pdf [accessed 8/31/16]

[239]   C. Xiao, "Update: XcodeGhost Attacker Can Phish Passwords and Open URLs Through Infected Apps", blog, 18 Sep.

2015;http://researchcenter.paloaltonetworks.com/2015/09/update-xcodeghost-attacker-can-phish-passwords-and-open-urls-though-infected-apps/ [accessed 8/31/16]

[240]   S. Poeplau et al, "Execute This! Analyzing Unsafe and Malicious Dynamic Code Loading in Android Applications", in Proceedings of the 2014 Network and Distributed System Security Symposium, 2014;http://www.internetsociety.org/doc/execute-analyzing-unsafe-and-malicious-dynamic-code-loading-android-applications [accessed 8/31/16]

[241]   J. Xie et al, "Hot or Not? The Benefits and Risks of iOS Remote Hot Patching", blog, 27 Jan. 2016; https://www.fireeye.com/blog/threat-research/2016/01/hot_or_not_the_bene.html [accessed 8/31/16]

[242]   M. Thompson, "Method Swizzling", blog, 17 Feb. 2014;http://nshipster.com/method-swizzling/ [accessed 8/31/16]